'Till Murder Do Us Part

Anthony David

Published by Trellis Publishing, 2021.

While every precaution has been taken in the preparation of this book, the publisher assumes no responsibility for errors or omissions, or for damages resulting from the use of the information contained herein.

'TILL MURDER DO US PART

First edition. July 1, 2021.

Copyright © 2021 Anthony David.

ISBN: 979-8224629312

Written by Anthony David.

'TILL MURDER DO US PART

ANTHONY DAVID

Always a Victim

Gaile Owens was not a very good murderer. In fact, few people could have made a worse job of hiring a killer to dispose of their abusive husband. She may have ended years of violence – physical and sexual but Owens, though, would pay a huge price for her inability to plan an undiscovered crime – a death sentence, a quarter of a century in prison and estrangement from her children.

Owens was released from prison in 2011, granted parole following a change of heart from her state Governor, but her incarceration was merely the latest, lengthy, instalment of a lifetime of suffering. Her story is a complex one, a tragedy of betrayal that reached Shakespearean proportions.

Marcia Gaile Owens was born on 22nd September 1952, the second child of Jewell and Izora Kirksey. Her father was a product of the era, a hard-working self-made man, who ran a service station and was trained as a mechanic. Not only was he hard working, but hard drinking as well; coming home drunk would often turn him into a violent wife and child beater.

The Kirkseys were fundamental Christians, members of the Calvary United Pentecostal Church. There, the pathways to Hell were laid out more readily than the roads to heaven. Gaile's older brother, Wilson, suffered from cerebral palsy, and the Church knew better than doctors how he should be treated. Purity in faith would lead to purity in body; all that Wilson needed to do was to achieve oneness with God, and his problems would go away. Time after time, the congregation would pray for a cure for young Wilson, they would lay hands upon his head. But still his palsy remained; and that was clearly the fault of the boy – his sin causing his problem. In fact, Wilson was of school age before he received any medical support for his condition.

But the Calvary United Pentecostal Church taught more than the consequences of sin and the results of a lack of absolute faith in God. It taught that the husband was the boss in a marriage, and a woman's role was to be completely subservient to her partner. It was a lesson that would have tragic consequences for Gaile in later years.

Jewell took that male right to dominance to extremes; beatings for Izora were commonplace, and so too was the use of the belt on Gaile and her younger sister Carolyn. 'At first I tried to stop (her husband) from doing that,' Izora later said 'but then Gaile just had to take her beating. She had to – I just got out of the way and she just had to take those beatings.'

Indeed, Izora's maternal instincts towards her daughter were not of the norm. She had a business of her own, and that took up much of her time. From her home, she ran a child care service, often catering for ten pre-school youngsters at a time. She sold her services on her ability to toilet train her young charges, and the Kirksey's small home featured a neatly arrayed line of potties resting in the hallway.

Because of her brother's illness, Gaile took on many of the responsibilities of the eldest child in a home. But one duty that was not a normal one for a child to perform was that of protector towards her mother. In fact, not only protector but also, at times, scapegoat.

Izora would often keep Gaile up with her, stopping her going to bed, to wait for Jewell's return from a drinking session. She knew that the man was less likely to beat her if their daughter was present. When the drunken 'head' of the family would finally fall into a snoring stupor, Izora would often steal money from his service station takings, removing the cash directly from the bag he carried. If the missing money was noticed, the consequences would be another, not unexpected, beating. Izora would make sure that it was Gaile who absorbed this heavy-handed punishment. It is fair to say that the young Gaile absorbed two lessons: firstly, stealing money was OK if there was no other way to get it and secondly, beatings were to be expected from men, and should remain secret.

If home was tough, the tendrils of the Calvary United Pentecostal Church spread into Gaile's school life as well. There were certain ways to behave, and certain ways to look. Hair should stay uncut; clothing should cover the entire body; the long dresses covering legs and arms. Swimming was out, even in the steaming air of Memphis; the notion of being close to a boy not permitted in any way. Unsurprisingly, these restrictions created a girl who was withdrawn and isolated. For all this, her grades were good, and her reports indicated a hard working, respectful girl with an excellent attitude.

For a while at least. Then, those As and Bs began to turn into Cs and Ds. The excellent attitude turned to just satisfactory. But there was a reason. And that reason was her uncle Marshall, her father's brother. While she was very young, Marshall seemed a perfect family relation. He doted on his niece, and she adored his company.

But then friendliness turned sinister, and the seven-year-old Gaile was scared and confused when his hands went inside her underwear. That abuse would continue, culminating in an attempted rape. Gaile told her mother, although Izora denied this. Marshall's attentions, though, were not limited to his niece. He lived, with his wife, on a rambling farm which had other tenants. When it was discovered that he was involved in a relationship with another minor, the marriage broke down.

However, not everything in young Gaile's life was negative. She was very close with her Aunt Nanny, Uncle Nicky and their two children, often spending the weekends with them, where she would count down the final hours before her return home, wishing that time could slow down until it stopped.

Nicky and Nanny were also church going folk, but their Presbyterian version was a different proposition to the Calvary United Pentecostal Church. Here Gaile discovered a loving, forgiving God. A God that allowed female worshippers to wear make up to His church. Gaile would be allowed nail varnish while staying with her Aunt and Uncle, and they would buy make up remover on their way back to

Gaile's home. Another secret to keep, although this time, one which she enjoyed.

As Gaile reached adolescence, she became increasingly introverted. Boys were denied to her, Jewell keeping a shotgun visible by the front door should any would be suitor call. But other things were changing for the better. The family's church gained a new preacher, one with more liberal rules, and it split with the strict Pentecostal Church. A result was that women's rights became more recognised. Another result of the new preacher's arrival was that Carolyn spent less and less time at home, and more and more time with the preacher's family. Gaile remained at home, and life continued much as before.

Then, as a young adult, she spent a night away from home. Jewell suspected her of experimenting with drugs, and made her, a young woman, strip in front of him. Although there was no evidence of drug taking, he beat her with his belt. It was enough, and Gaile moved out of the family home and took an apartment.

She found a job, working at a Children's Medical Centre, and began to gain some independence and confidence. Then, at work, she met the man for whom she would eventually pay to be murdered. Ron Owens lived a classic split existence. On the surface, he seemed the perfect gentleman, in private, he was a monster.

Whatever, to young Gaile he was a man to whom she was in awe. At just twenty, she was overwhelmed that an older man, experienced with life, could be interested in her. He was a Vietnam veteran, where he had served as a medic.

His often-told story modestly reflected his heroism. 'I stood up twice in Vietnam,' he would self deprecatingly claim 'and was shot both times.' Ron Owens was the centre of social gatherings, amusing friends and associates with anecdotes and jokes; he was immaculate in appearance, a tidy, organised and controlled man who seemed, on the face of it, the diametric opposite of her father and his abusive family.

But we know that, whether subconsciously or not, men with a penchant for domestic violence find woman who have been through such horrors. And those women, in turn, seem to become attracted to this kind of man. Owens did not control himself, but wanted a woman who would submit fully to his wishes.

Gaile had remained a virgin, and was sexually naïve. She was unaware of how attractive she was, since she had been brought up to hide her body. and be embarrassed by it. She could not believe that a sporting, gregarious man such as Ron Owens could be in love with her. Indeed, she turned down his first proposal, saying that she would need to think about it, so unlikely had the invitation seemed to her.

But Ron was persistent, and Gaile accepted his second request for her hand. All seemed fine until their wedding night. Gaile was embarrassed about her body, and nervous about consummating the marriage. Ron wanted the light on, and was physically rough with his inexperienced new wife. She found the act painful and unpleasant, he told her that she 'frigid', and threatened that if she did not satisfy him, he would seek physical gratification elsewhere. It would be a regular threat, one to which totally believed was her own fault.

The Owens' life continued on two levels – on the surface, an almost Disney-esque picture of domestic bliss; Gaile the housewife with the immaculate home, Ron studying for his chosen profession. Socially, a popular man with his petite, perfect, wife. Under the surface, though, tensions continued to rise.

A year after their marriage, Gaile fell pregnant. Ron was furious, feeling that they were not financially able to start a family. Beyond the closed doors of home, however, the act of the beaming, delighted father to be was played to perfection. Following the birth of their son, Stephen, at the beginning of 1973, the façade was maintained. Gaile took a job and the image of domestic bliss was projected onto those who knew them. But underneath the thin varnish was a woman unable to control her post pregnancy weight, who was desperately taking pills to keep her waistline trim. A woman downtrodden by her sexually demanding husband, one who has emotionally stunted by his criticism and demands.

Despite her work, they had no money and Gaile eventually stole funds from the surgery in which she worked. As would later be the case with her much more serious crime, she was not a good criminal, and was quickly caught. She had to pay back the money she had taken, and did so with a loan from her mother, working in her day care business to pay it back.

Any anger Ron displayed towards his wife's stupid actions was hypocritical. Later, it would emerge that he was not a war hero, in fact he had never even been in Vietnam. More than this, he had lied about his qualifications to get a job, claiming a full Bachelor's degree, when in fact he had just an associate's nursing qualification.

Indeed, lying and deceit were close companions to Ron Owens. He carried out his threat to find gratification outside of his marriage, and over the years had several affairs. He was not even particularly secretive about them, and to Gaile these liaisons represented the biggest threat to the candied existence they pretended to live.

More evidence of Ron's mistreatment of his wife occurred the day before she was due to have her second child, by C Section. They had been out to dinner, and afterwards Ron insisted on sex despite her being nine months pregnant and suffering from frequent, intense abdominal pains; the damage he did led their bed being blood soaked. It seems likely that the hospital findings of the separation of the placenta from her abdominal wall was caused by the attempted intercourse.

But this complex scenario was becoming even more tangled. Gaile twice more forged her way to stealing money from employers, the first time going to prison. On the second occasion, following her release from prison, she had been employed by a friend of Ron, a church connection. He did not press charges.

This continual stealing, combined with a self-confessed difficulty in maintaining the truth was considered by many to be a part of a wider personality or mental health disorder, such as compulsive obsessive disorder. Her brother in law, a doctor, said:

'She was a good person, but she was sort of a pathological liar...sometimes you couldn't hardly believe what she said.' Unfortunately, Carolyn, his wife, would be far less balanced in her conclusions.

But Gaile Owens did try to move her life forwards. When her husband was appointed associate director of nursing at The Baptist Memorial Hospital in Memphis – a role that caused him to travel a lot – she took up some extra classes at a local college.

The couple were in financial disarray, paying back money Gaile had stolen, looking after two children, maintaining the lifestyle that appeared perfect on the surface. However, on looking more deeply, it was easy to observe discomforting traits in Ron. His humour was frequently at the expense of his wife, which she to take in good heart; he once bought a penis shaped birthday cake for a work colleague, which went down very badly at the hospital in which he worked.

Another matter not well received by his work colleagues was Ron's affair with a young nurse. Perhaps the news, which she must have known about as she had mysterious phone calls and even a message cut from newspaper, caused her latest misdemeanour. She began once again to embezzle funds from her workplace. Yet again, she was quickly caught and forced to leave. Another bill hit the family's depleted funds, which Gaile's parents paid by taking out a mortgage on their own home, and also selling some property they rented out. The $20,000 debt they incurred stretched their own finances tightly.

But the money situation in the Owens' household was even worse. Somewhat bizarrely, given her record with money, she was in charge of paying bills, which she did not do. Debts mounted, and warning letters came and were ignored. Once again, the dichotomy in Gaile's life showed itself. To many, she was the charming wife and mother, the perfect hostess who was popular among friends from her church. But to others, particularly friends of Ron, she was the cause of the family difficulties.

Gaile was frustrated by her husband's latest infidelity. She followed him to work, and confronted him with his illicit girlfriend. The result? Ron slapped her, threw her against their car, and accused her of spying on him.

The bills were completely out of control, her abusive husband was having yet another affair, their picture perfect home was about to be repossessed. In her panicked mind, it seemed inevitable that not only was the veneer thin life she had created about to be lost, but when the house went, so would Ron; he would, she was sure, take her sons with him.

She considered her options, suicide among them. Then, the day after the confrontation, Gaile made her biggest mistake of all. Like most big US cities, there are districts of Memphis which are more sinister than the middle-class enclave in which the Owens lived. Gaile drove to one of these, a down trodden part of the city called Bearwater.

This run-down area was all black in the 1980s, a location where most locals were employed in either the local steel mill, or the Firestone Tyre plant. Despite its predominance of Afro-Americans, it was an area frequented by white people, either travelling past the basic housing on their way to the city centre, or sometimes looking for supplies of drugs.

So, despite the newish upmarket Buick Gaile drove (another ill affordable part of the pretence of gracious living), she did not look too much out of place. At least to begin with. But as time and her visits continued, local men began to realise that she could be tapped for money. For the area, big sums. Promise to kill her husband, and the money was yours. Such promises did not need to be honoured.

Christmas throws families together. Usually that is for good, but where tensions exist, the high spirits of children, the pressure of everybody closed in together, make Christmas become one of the most demanding times for families. Maybe things became even worse in Christmas of 1984; perhaps money issues meant the children could not get gifts in vogue, the ones their mates would be receiving. Whether this was the case or not, it was shortly after the big day in that year that Gaile Owens once more visited Bearwater, and matters took on a more serious tinge.

Later, 'Bubba' Sykes gave his view on what was going on. He was a convicted murderer and drug dealer, but now, like the other men she approached, he simply saw the chance for easy money from an apparently naïve but rich woman. Little did they men know that she had no more money then them.

'Here's a rich woman come down in the ghetto,' he said 'and she starts talking to guys on the corner trying to nickel up to get a bottle of wine. She's offering them big money. Anybody in my neighbourhood would have told her "Sure, I'll do it."'

As a person planning a murder, Gaile could not really have been more inept. She asked so many men to do the deed, many of whom agreed, took the money and did no more. She went as far as handing over a picture of her husband, and drawing a map of her house. She took a group of men, Sykes included, to see her church and her neighbourhood. Places where to see a group of rough looking black men would turn heads, especially in the company of one of their own. Meanwhile, the men were continuing to exploit the situation. They took $500 – all she claimed to have left; they blackmailed her over the map and picture of Ron, threatening to tell the police.

In fact, they also started to get fed up with her. As good a source of ready cash as she might be, they became wearied by her persistence. By the never-ending stories of her 'bad marriage' and by her demands that one of them kill her husband.

It was as she was tiring the men out that she met Sidney Porterfield. He ran a shop in the district, and was also a friend of Sykes. She did the normal act, telling Porterfield that she wanted her husband to be killed, and asking whether he would do it. Later, Porterfield said that she offered him $17000 to commit the murder.

The murder that would see both Porterfield and Gaile Owens sentenced to death happened on February 17th 1985. It was a Sunday. The family attended the morning Church Service at the Abundant Life church, with Gaile singing as always in the choir. Later, she and her sons joined her sister for lunch. Meanwhile, Ron went to play golf with his friend Keith Ferguson.

It is worth noting at this point that it was Ferguson, Owens' best friend, who offered much of the damning criticism of Gaile. He denied ever seeing evidence of violence from Ron, and he also defended his extra marital dalliances as being the only part of Ron's life that was satisfying for him.

After lunch was over, Gaile drove into Memphis and collected Porterfield, who did not own a car. However, she asked Porterfield to check out her home, so he could work out Ron's movements. She also told him that she could not pay him until the following week. Porterfield said he would borrow a car, and do so. It was almost as though both parties were putting off the attack, as though they were happy to plan it, but not carry it out. Gaile arrived back to her home in Bartlett in time for choir practice at 4.30pm.

It was normal for the men, including Ron, to play basketball after the evening service, and for the boys (Brian and Stephen) to watch him. But this particular Sunday was different. Firstly, another church had booked the court, and it meant that their church would get less time playing than normal. Ron decided to call it off, but Gail worked hard to persuade him to stay and play. Secondly, she was insistent that the boys could not watch him on this occasion, although they pleaded with her. Instead, she took them for a take away, where they met up with some of the other mothers, and then went on to Carolyn's home. There they played games, much later than normal especially considering it was a school night. At about 10.30 they headed for home.

It was Stephen, not yet in his teens, who discovered his father. There were clues that all was not well; doors left open, the car abandoned, chairs lying on the floor. Ron was unconscious, and bleeding profusely from the hammering he had received with a tyre iron. He died in the early hours of the next morning.

Gaile was due to collect in excess of $100000 insurance money, and she would need it. When the news of her husband's murder made the inside pages of the local newspaper, it was picked up by George James, one of the men she had tried to get to kill Ron. He immediately contacted her, demanding money to keep silent. But she had no ready cash, and asked him to wait. James was determined to get his money, and immediately. He contacted the police ready to tell his tale in order to get a reward. With the authorities now listening in, he contacted Gaile once more, and insisted on money, while she once again told him he would need to wait.

They arranged a meeting, and James, wired and observed by the nearby police, tried to get her to identify the killer. 'I don't know what's going on, or who did it or anything,' she said.

But she soon caved in to police, admitting that she had offered money for Ron's killing. She identified Porterfield, but told police that she had not followed through with her plan, or paid him.

She told police that Ron had been cruel towards her, but those childhood years with its influence of church and a violent home skewed the ways she saw things. 'We've just had a bad marriage over the years, and I just felt like he had...mentally I just felt like he had been cruel to me. There was very little physical violence,' she told officers.

Porterfield proved as inept at crime as Gaile, explaining away the murder as a kind of self defence when Ron grabbed him and tried to drag him inside. The explanation overlooked various pieces of evidence, such as the location of Ron's sports bag, which made it clear the killing had happened inside the house. Detective K.D. Wray, in charge of solving the crime, had an open and shut case.

For Gaile, it was. At no point did she portray anything except remorse, and at no point did she deny seeking to pay someone to kill her husband. As much as it shocked the community, who had been drawn into the lie that was their life, her church friends had to accept that Gaile had planned the crime.

For Porterfield, though, things were different. As suspicious as his confession was, the police knew that people often confessed to things that they had not done. They had no DNA evidence linking him to the crime.

A plea bargain was organised. If both perpetrators accepted their guilt, they would escape the death penalty. However, both needed to do so. Gaile accepted the offer, but Porterfield and his team thought that they could win a trial. The offer was withdrawn.

It soon became apparent to Gaile's attorneys that she had a defence; she was clearly a victim of domestic abuse, particularly sexual violence. Whether she would be believed – the words of a convicted fraudster made against an upstanding member of the community, and (as was believed at the time) war hero – was another matter. It was a test that would never come to be taken.

Gaile insisted, for the sake of her children and for the shame she felt at failing to satisfy her husband's perverse desires, that she would not testify as to what had taken place in the confines of her home. The mental cruelty, the affairs, the occasional physical violence and the depravity of what Ron had insisted on in the bedroom – those were not things to share in front of the courtroom and the media.

Her strict church upbringing, where woman were taught to be subordinate to the whims of men, and the violence she had witnessed and experienced from her own father, had instilled in her an unwillingness to discuss such matters, even when her life was dependent on it. Interestingly, her sister felt the same, refusing to defend Gaile in court, and Gaile too refusing to allow her to do so.

Further, this was the mid-1980s, a time when America still did not widely recognise the crime of marital rape. The Judge, Joseph McCartie, was unsympathetic, denying the defence the funding to carry out expert investigations into Gaile's situation. The defence team attempted to bring into court evidence of Ron's affairs; the police had discovered letters between he and one of his lovers. However, Assistant District Attorney general Don Strother, in charge of the prosecution, denied that any such letter existed; they would only come to light many years later, and the defence were denied the chance to present such evidence. It was a deceit that Strother had employed at other times in different cases, including preventing the jury from seeing an x-ray that proved a shooting could not have come from the accused's gun. The man in that case, Philip Workman, was executed.

Strother denied such allegations.

And so, the trial took place, the jury hearing only part of the story. Gaile refused to testify, but her son, Stephen, just 12 at this point, was forced to. He could not meet his mother's eye. No news of the beatings, of the affairs, of Gaile's abusive upbringing, of the sexual depravity in which she was forced to participate was presented to the jury. They were not told that she had been offered, and accepted, a plea bargain – the Judge ensured that no news of this came out. Her defence team, unprepared, under-funded and frequently changed, were ineffective. If ever there was a case of a male dominated system disregarding the horrors of abusive marriages, this was it. It took the jury just seventy minutes to convict her. Porterhouse was also convicted, and would die on Death Row many years later.

Gaile was denied all access to her sons. They were taken in by her sister, who perhaps because of her husband's close friendship with Ron, and because she too had been through the tainting experiences of her early childhood, abandoned her sister, acting for the prosecution at the trial. It seems that letters to the boys were intercepted, and telephone calls denied. Her pastor at the Abundant Life Church also made clear his support for Carolyn and the boys over Gaile.

As with all convicts on Death Row, Gaile's case underwent multiple reviews; but each time new findings were ignored or dismissed, with the Judiciary demonstrating a markedly ignorant regard for the impact of domestic abuse on a victim. Ultimately, her death sentence was set for September 28th, 2010; she would be the first woman to be executed in Tennessee for two centuries.

Following an enormous campaign to reveal the truth – her execution could put women's rights back decades – Governor Phil Bredesen commuted the death penalty to life imprisonment. That meant that she was able to apply for parole. Even then, two men on the panel voted against her release, but she won by four votes to two.

As an adult, away from his Aunt's influence, Stephen reunited with his mother. Today, the two are close like any mother and son. Well, perhaps not any mother. Gaile Owens is a victim beyond what most would ever fear to endure. A victim of an intolerant Pentecostal Church, a victim of an abusive father, a victim of a mother who would not stand up to her, a victim of a husband who was mentally cruel, sexually violent and a liar, a victim of a court system that was frightening in its disregard for the rights of woman and a victim of a society that demands sugary evidence of success but has little interest in truth.

SHE KILLED THE PREACHER

John Fontaine

The Case of Mary Winkler

Mary Winkler, at first appearances, would seem to be an altogether normal woman. So too did her family, with a husband who was a Church minister and three young children, girls aged just eight, six and one.

The family lived in Selmer, Tenn., a small town occupied by around 4,500 people, according to the 2015 census. The town is situated to the south west of the state. Not much has happened in Selmer; the most famous person to have been born there was Chad Harville, former pitcher for the Oakland A's, and for one year, the Red Sox. He achieved a 4-9 win-loss record over his career in the MLB.

Today, the most famous- or infamous- person to have come from Selmer is Mary Winkler. In 2006, Mary sparked a border-crossing manhunt, and a court case followed nationwide. She had killed her husband with a shot to the back from the family's shotgun. But it was the gripping, and at times bizarre, court case which gripped the attention of the nation.

Matthew dead, Mary and the family Missing

The date was March 6th, 2007. It was a Tuesday like any other. Mary and Matthew were at home all day together, although Matthew was due to give a sermon that evening.

It was actually members of Matthew's congregation who found his body that night. They had visited his home to check up on him after he had missed the service he was set to give; instead, they found him lying dead, having been shot in the back.

There was no sign of Mary or any of their children at the home, and as such, they were reported missing. The authorities quickly sent out an Amber Alert, since nobody had any idea what could have happened to them, or where they might be. Family and friends had no information to provide police on their whereabouts.

There was every chance that the family had been kidnapped or murdered, and their bodies disposed of elsewhere, although police could not identify a break in, and had no reason to believe that anything of value had been stolen.

It was only a day later that she was arrested in Alabama, having run from the family home with her young children. They were found 350 miles away from home, at Orange Beach, and in the back seat of the van was the family's shotgun. It was certainly suspicious; but what reason could Mary have possibly had for committing such a crime?

The Trial

In the build up to the case going to trial, public interest ramped up. Speculation had been rife about why Mary would have murdered her husband, a seemingly nice, well respected member of the local community. Perhaps either one of them had had an affair, and Matthew had been killed in a crime of passion. Or maybe he had been killed for an insurance claim?

As such, the press reported every step of the story as it came out during the hearing. The trial began when a Tennessee Bureau of Investigation Agent John Mehr read a statement that Mary had made very soon after her arrest. In it, Mary claimed that the couple had been arguing about their family finances, before Mary had shot her husband with their 12 gauge shotgun. She had said that the last thing she had wanted was to actually murder her husband, but she had been brandishing the gun in an effort to convince him to work through their problems, together. The argument had been ongoing throughout the day, and Mary had finally snapped, resorting to drastic measures to be able to convince him. She had never intended to kill him: she had said in the statement, 'I don't want this at all. I don't want any of this to be, at all.'

The statement continued on, and Mary claimed that they had argued often and argued fiercely. 'He had really been on me lately,' Mary had said, 'criticizing me for things- the way I walk, I eat, everything. It was just building up to a point. I was tired of it. I guess I got to a point and snapped.'

At first glance, it would seem that Mary had simply lost her composure, become angry, and killed her husband 'as the red mist had descended'. But after their initial statement, Mary's attorney indicated that there was much more that would come out about Matthew's behaviour when she testified which would help to explain her actions. Clearly, there were more problems with their marriage than the occasional, albeit fierce, argument.

Mary's Crime

The case for the prosecution wasted no time in painting Mary as a cold blooded killer, who left her husband to die without remorse. Admittedly, the plain facts of the case made Mary seem unbelievably guilty. The prosecution relied on several of these facts in their attempt to convince the jury of Mary's guilt for the charge of murder.

Mary had disconnected the phone immediately after she shot her husband, stopping him from being able to call the emergency services, or receive any calls that may have come in. This suggested that Mary had been in full control of her actions, not panicking, since it is unlikely that somebody in a state of anxiety would think to disconnect the phone.

The fact that Mary had attempted to flee to Orange Beach, Alabama, was also a key point for the prosecution. Immediately after Matthew's death, Mary had taken the family minivan to the beach, with her three children. Later on in her defence, Mary would claim that she ran because '[n]obody would believe me, and they'd take the girls away and put me away.' Certainly, in many murder cases, the fact that the defendant flees the scene is a certain indicator of guilt.

The family's daughter Patricia testified that she couldn't understand her mother's actions. All that she knew was that she had heard a 'big boom', and the sound of something heavy hitting the floor. She quickly ran to the bedroom to see her father on the floor, and her mother holding the shotgun. She had no idea what could possibly have provoked her mother to shoot him.

Another sticking point was that the family finances had been 'in shambles' just before the murder had taken place. This had led Mary to become embroiled in what is called a 'check kiting' scam. In it, she had received checks from unidentified accounts in Canada and Nigeria, and had ultimately fallen to a financial scam that had lost the family money. Prosecutors claimed that this could have somehow instigated the argument that led to Matthew's death, and that Mary had felt as if she had no way out of the scam.

They also jumped on the fact that in an initial conversation with investigators, Mary had told them that their marriage was a happy one, and that '[t]here's no poor me. I'm in control.' They clearly wanted to paint a picture of Mary as remorseless, deceitful, and smarter than she looked.

The Cross-examination

During her cross-examination in court, Mary stated that she didn't remember grabbing the gun from the closet in which it was kept. What she did remember was that 'something went off', 'hearing a loud boom', and that 'it wasn't as loud as I thought it would be.' She did admit that she had shot her husband. Matthew rolled from the bed- upon which he had been lying as they had argued- and dropped to the floor. Mary described smelling gunpowder.

Prosecutor Walter Freeland asked her whether she understood that 'pulling a trigger is what makes it go boom', to which she replied that she did.

Matthew asked her why she had snapped and shot him. She could only say 'I'm sorry.' The shotgun blast had been inflicted from behind, directly into Matthew's back, and had caused severe damage to his organs and spine. According to prosecutors, he had in fact still been alive as Mary had run from the house.

But these simple facts were far from the end of the story, as Mary was to reveal.

Appearances and Revelations

At first, Mary spoke of her husband not in the past tense, but in the present, as if she couldn't quite understand how final her actions really had been. In reminiscing about happier times, Mary told the court that her husband was an intelligent, social man, and that the family had shared many 'good times' together. She also seemed to enjoy talking about her children, and the happiness they brought her.

This happy family life, however, was simply one side of the marriage. Mary's attorney stated that '[w]hat went on behind their closed doors is going to have to be told ... Some of what we've got from the state of Tennessee touches on sexual abuse.' Their defence was that Matthew had made Mary's life a 'living hell': '[w]e will show you proof that he would destroy objects that she loved, he would isolate her from her family and he would abuse her not just verbally, not just emotional and not just physically—in other ways, too.'

Just before the murder, Mary claimed that Matthew had been threatening their children and even attempted to throttle their infant daughter, Breanna. He had been shouting, angry, because he had wanted a son. As the case went on, it became obvious that this was only the tip of the iceberg, however, and more and more sordid details of their home life would come to light.

Matthew, Mary claimed, was a violent, abusive husband. Shortly after their marriage, he ordered her to stop socialising with any of her family and friends (a common tactic among abusive spouses in order to further isolate their partners from potential help). Winkler's sisters described how Mary seemed stuck in her marriage, unhappy, but unable to leave. In an interview, they said that 'As the years went on, she seemed to be nervous to show love towards us.'

Mary was commonly 'screamed and hollered' at by her husband. 'He just flailed. He's a big guy and he was just all over ... He'd point his finger inches away from my nose. Whatever he was upset about, it was my fault,' Mary had said. It could be over anything: 'I was fat, my hair wasn't right, the girls, if something went wrong, it was my fault. I didn't know when it was coming.' Mary described her situation as one familiar to abused wives and husbands across America.

Her attorney, Steve Farese, provided further information based on his conversations with Mary. She had needed her husband's permission for everything, even for getting her hair cut. 'This was constant, and she lived a life where she walked on eggshells.' This abuse, he said, had given Mary symptoms of post traumatic stress disorder, simply because 'she didn't know what was going to happen next.' Furthermore, a psychologist testified as part of Mary's defence, saying that her symptoms were those of clinical depression and PTSD.

During her time on the stand, Mary also claimed that Matthew had forced her to watch pornography with him, and that he had bought her several 'slutty' costumes for sex, which she normally would never have worn, but for fear of her husband. If she refused, Matthew wouldn't hesitate to get physical, hitting her or even using his belt to whip her. Mary famously produced a wig and a pair of white high heels in the witness box during her cross-examination to show the court evidence of Matthew's other side.

Mary stated that she was never happy watching pornography, dressing up in sexy outfits or performing the sex acts that Matthew wanted. She went along with his ideas, however, because she didn't dare face his reaction if she didn't. 'I'd just do anything to help him stay happy.' Throughout these revelations, Mary was visibly embarrassed and uncomfortable. Clearly she would have preferred that none of them had ever come to light; but Mary felt it necessary to brave what her neighbors, and the nation, might think in order to clear her name and justify her actions.

Mary's family had been quick to corroborate her side of the story. Her father, Clark Freeman, had spoken out through Good Morning America and detailed the 'physical, mental, verbal' abuse that his daughter had suffered. Other friends came forward during the court case, and gave similar verdicts on their relationship. A friend of Mary's, Rudie Thomsen, said that '[o]ne Sunday, Mary came into the church and I looked at her and she had a black eye.' Similarly, Mary's friend Amy Redmon agreed that Matthew had been controlling: '[h]e was an authority figure, and he made the decisions basically. It was obvious.'

Conversely, Matthew's family denied that their son had been anything like Mary had depicted in her defence testimony. Matthew's father, Charles Daniel Winkler, said that his son was a kind, gentle man, who could have done nothing to justify what the defence was claiming. Diane spoke several times during the trial, lashing out at Mary: 'You've never told your girls you're sorry! Don't you think you at least owe them that?'

The dramatic story of a supposedly kindly, gentle church minister having such a sordid, cruel and abusive hidden life gripped America. The case was covered extensively on all major networks, discussed on late night panel shows

The Jury's Verdict

While the prosecutors had tried to convince the jury to convict her on a charge of first degree murder, they were unsuccessful. The jury came to their verdict by April, that year. It took them eight hours to deliberate their way to the decision; this mirrored the response of the nation, which was similarly undecided on just what punishment Mary really deserved.

Mary was found guilty of voluntary manslaughter, a charge which carries a far more lenient sentence than murder. While murderers can receive full life sentences, and in certain states receive the death penalty, the maximum sentence for voluntary manslaughter is only 6 years.

Mary showed little emotion at the verdict, but did embrace each of her relatives afterwards. In a show of support, her family had been sat in the row behind her, and all linked arms with one another to demonstrate their solidarity. Afterwards, she was taken back into custody to await sentencing.

Mary's attorney stated afterwards that Mary's testimony had been central in securing the more lenient sentence. 'I think Mary's testimony was integral in this decision. They had to hear it from Mary', Farese told the press. 'They judged her credibility and they saw that she had an abusive relationship and they made their judgment based upon that.'

For Mary, the most important implication of the verdict was that she could finally begin to think of being reunited with her children. Speaking on her behalf after the trial, Farese continued: 'We would like to do so many things to open up communication between Mary and the paternal grandparents and to get the children out of this cycle of constant upheaval over this terrible tragic event.' But the question of how long she would be in prison remained.

Mary's sentencing was scheduled for May 18th, at which point both Mary and the prosecution would have a final chance to address the court before the judge decided on the final jail term. However, the situation looked positive for Mary. Not only would the five months that she had been imprisoned awaiting trial be taken into consideration, but the judge had indicated that alternatives to incarceration would be on the table. Perhaps Mary could avoid jail time altogether.

Sentencing: The Trial at an End

Due to a scheduling error, the hearing took place around three weeks late, on June 8th.

Mary took to the stand one last time to plead for mercy. She read aloud from a prepared statement, telling Matthew's family of her sorrow and remorse for her actions. She was 'so sorry that this had happened', and would 'always miss and love' her husband. 'I ask for mercy and understanding, but I know whatever decision you reach today will be right ... I ask you to please let me go home today and be with my children.' Tabitha Freeman- Mary's sister- had also pleaded for leniency, in particular to let Mary be reunited with her children. She went as far as calling Mary 'the best example of a good person I can think of'.

Members of Matthew's family, too, took to the stand to plead their case for the prosecution. Charles and his wife were clearly hurt and in disbelief at Mary's actions both in murdering their son, and believed that Mary had purposefully smeared his name at trial. 'The monster that you have painted for the world to see? I don't think that monster existed,' Diane Winkler had said.

After speaking their pieces, all that Mary, her family, and Matthew's parents could do was wait until the judge's decision. The trial- as well as the very public 'trial' that Mary had been through in the media- was finally at an end.

The defence had requested that Mary be granted full probation, or judicial diversion, both outcomes which would have meant that Mary would spent no further time in prison, and even that her record would be cleared of wrongdoing altogether. This request was denied.

After recess, Mary was told that she would spend 3 years in prison for her crime. But Circuit Judge J. Weber McCraw reduced that amount to just 210 days total in prison before she would be allowed to leave on probation. She also had that sentence reduced further, due to the fact that she had spent five months incarcerated waiting for trial.

Moreover, that time would be spent not in jail, but in a mental health centre in Tennessee. There, she would receive treatment for both her depression and post traumatic stress disorder. After such a long ordeal, with the prosecution fighting to either put Mary on death row or to imprison her indefinitely, it seemed that she had gotten off with hardly a slap on the wrist.

Steve Farese branded the sentence 'a victory': '[s]he could be in prison for life, and that's what everybody thought she was headed for to begin with.' Her other attorney, Leslie Ballin, said '[s]he'll be able to get out and fight the battle she wants to, and that is to get her children back.' Mary could finally think about the future again.

But certain signs indicated that it would not be as easy to reconcile with her children and family as she might hope. Matthew's family left the courtroom without making a comment to the press, as did the prosecution, clearly disappointed in the verdict. They gave no indication that they would be happy to open dialogue about Mary's daughters- not with the woman whom they believed to have murdered their son in cold blood.

The aftermath of Mary's release

Mary was released on August 14th, 2007. She had only been sentenced the previous June.

Upon her release, her lawyer informed the press that Mary would not be speaking with them, to maintain her privacy. During her time in the mental health facility, Mary could finally begin her attempt to win full custody of her three daughters, and she was still fighting this case at the time of her release. She had not seen her children, apart from Patricia's brief testimony as part of the case, for over a year. Throughout the case, and after Mary's release, her children were staying with Matthew's family.

Moreover, she was still fighting a $2 million dollar civil lawsuit filed by Matthew's parents. They also took legal measures, which, if successful, would have meant that the custody of Mary's children remained with them.

After her release, Mary seemed happier to her family and friends. From an outside perspective, it could be easy to claim that this was just as much due to her happiness at avoiding a jail sentence as it was to her being rid of an abuser. She was in fact living with friends at first after her release, and went back to work at a dry cleaners in McMinnville, Tenn., 200 miles from Selmer.

In the same interview as was mentioned before, Mary's sisters agreed that she had changed entirely. After years of shyness, Mary seeming unable or unwilling to show love to them for fear of her husband's violence, she seemed to finally be able to open up. 'Now it's back to the old Mary [who] loves us and doesn't care to come and hug us and gives us a kiss on the cheek.'

Since then, Mary lived in McMinnville. She has moved between jobs, working at the dry cleaners, before starting work at a nursery. She briefly dated the brother of one of her most vocal supporters, Paul Pillow; afterwards, she moved in with Wayne Cantrell, a preacher living in Smithville nearby.

Mary regained custody of her three children in 2008, but by 2010, received the news that she had multiple sclerosis. Her diagnosis came at the worst time, as she was settling down in her new life; she had not long started medical school with the desire to become a nurse, and had to quit since the work would be too demanding. She hasn't returned to work since.

One comfort for Mary was that Matthew's parents seemed close to being able to forgive her. After her diagnosis, they gave Mary some time off from parenting by taking care of the children for a weekend, which soon turned into several months. Daniel Winkler has preached several times since the events on the topic of forgiveness, although when asked by local press why he chose the topic, he has refused to answer, presumably preferring to keep those details private.

Mary, too, preferred to put the past behind her. In an interview with WAFF 48, the NBC affiliate in Huntsville AL., she stated how she would prefer to stay out of the limelight, particularly for the sake of her girls. 'Whatever reason people have any problem with me, that's fine. Everybody's entitled to their opinion, but these girls are treated for who they are, not because of what their mother's done ... They're three very fine young ladies'.

Concluding Thoughts

Some members of the public reacted with disgust at the abnormally short sentence that Mary was given, and questioned whether a husband would have been given the same leniency as Mary was. Men's rights activist Glenn Sacks publicly questioned whether a man would have been shown such leniency, and pointed to the case of Scott Peterson (who received the death penalty for the murder of his pregnant wife) to indicate that no, a man would not. He also argued that the idea of abuse had been widened to include simple criticism, and should therefore not necessarily be used as defence of murder.

Conversely, there have been many women put in prison for murdering their abusive husbands, some for much longer than Mary Winkler. The 'battered woman defense', or the preferred terminology today of 'battering and its effects', is not a genuine legal defence in itself; it can, however, be used to convince a court of diminished responsibility. Its effectiveness is due to the sympathy that it elicits from jurors, who can be convinced that abuse is a form of provocation, and the murder a form of self defense. Under this defense, Mary's short sentence makes sense.

The case has remained a touch stone with regards to spousal abuse in the U.S. A made-for-TV movie, 'The Pastor's Wife', was released in 2011. It was based on the book of the same title, written by Dianne Fanning, an award winning crime writer. The story was changed somewhat, with the inclusion of a financial subplot involving tax fraud. However, it also made use of real life interviews with people who knew the Winklers- including Matthew's parents. His mother revealed that she could never believe Mary's story. Charles admitted that Mary's story could be true, and that he could forgive her if she confessed her purposeful intention to murder Matthew.

As for the community in which the family had lived, the reaction was largely one of forgiveness. According to members of that community, the town's 'Christian roots and ... its tendency to give people the benefit of the doubt' meant that they took Mary at her word. Mary's quite life in McMinnville and Smithville similarly shows that the American public would rather leave her and her family alone after their painful ordeal.

TRACEY GRISSOM

Claiming to be a victim of rape and other abuses, a distraught Tracey Grissom would travel to her ex-husband Hunter's workplace and shoot him six times in the back, receiving a twenty-five-year life sentence for his murder.

Her defense attorney would argue that Tracey was motivated by post-traumatic stress disorder caused by her Hunter's constant abuse and sexual assaults. One jury member had even asked the judge to be lenient in her sentencing as they were not allowed to hear details of her Hunter's alleged abuses (beatings, rape, sodomy).

But what really happened in the years that led up to May 15th, 2012? Was she in fact the victim of years of abuse by a psychotic husband? Or did she want to cash in on his $100,000 life insurance policy?

INSTANT ATTRACTION

The couple would meet during a dinner party in 2003 in Tuscaloosa, Alabama. Tracey was twenty-one years old and going through a divorce. She had a son, James Michael, from the previous marriage.

Family and friends would describe the union as "love at first sight." Hunter was blown away by the young Tracey's blue eyes and facial beauty.

"For him, it was love at first sight," crime author William Phelps said. "She was gorgeous."

A whirlwind courtship would ensue and the couple would elope in 2004.

"In the beginning, it was good," Tracey told CBS' 48 hours. "We had a friendship. Just your normal, honeymoon phase marriage."

"He was fun," Tracey said. "And he was attractive."

Hunter was two years younger than Tracey, however, and his mother felt that he had jumped the gun too early in the relationship.

Her words proved to be prophetic as after only eight months into the marriage, the marriage went south.

According to Tracey, their marital problems began with Hunter's drug addiction.

"I had caught him smoking marijuana," Tracey said. "Doing illegal things could cause a problem and I couldn't risk losing my son over."

Tracey claimed that she threatened her new spouse with a divorce but Hunter gave her his word that he would stop with his drug use. She stated that the relationship improved and the decided to start a construction company together.

"I took out an equity line to start a company," Tracey said. "Which was Grissom Construction. It was all in my name."

Hunter specialized in building elaborate boat docks. He had an artistic eye and could do docks, stairs, and other accouterments. The business began to grow in short order.

"They're going to take on the world," Phelps said. "They're going to be entrepreneurs and they're gonna make it."

They then had a daughter of their own, Anna Grace. The child was a long time coming for the couple. They had been trying for a long time as Tracey had five miscarriages before Anna Grace was born.

"She was premature," Tracey recalled. "Her heart and lungs were not developed. A very stressful time."

Behind closed doors things were rocky. On the surface, however, things looked good. They had a young family and were making money.

"All-American family," Phelps said. "White-picket fence. The whole nine yards. Middle-class. Suburbia. Maybe the Prince Charming that she's been waiting for."

But again, this was only on the surface. Tracey harbored secrets of her own. One of which was her own addiction to prescription drugs.

"Psychologically, there's something going on here," Phelps said. "There's something going on behind those beautiful eyes and it ain't good."

Tracey would often turn on on the children, showing off her temper. Then she would turn on Hunter.

"This would cause friction in the marriage," Phelps said. "And where there's friction, there's fire."

SETTING THE STAGE

Tracey would later state that Hunter would "act strangely" shortly before she filed divorce. She was a registered nurse and gave him an over-the-counter drug test. According to her, Hunter tested posted for marijuana, Oxycontin, opiates, and methamphetamine.

Hunter would later be arrested for marijuana possession but his family would insist that he never did the harder drugs.

Tracey would file for divorce in the summer of 2010 after six years of marriage. According to her, this would prompt physical abuse from Hunter.

Hunter had to move out but their divorce agreement would allow him access to the home.

"In September of 2010," Tracey recalled. "That was the first time he physically hit me. It (the abuse) got progressively worse. He had made the comments that if I told anybody he would kill me. I believed him."

Hunter' co-workers and family members would have a different take on the situation, however. His co-workers remembered a time when she tracked him down at one of the jobs and made a scene.

"She's screaming, jumping on him," Hunter's co-worker said. "Said something about him having another girlfriend and used the expression about, 'You are mine. I'll kill you. I'll kill you. You are mine."

"She's borderline demonic," Hunter's mother said. " mean, I absolutely believe—that she is that troubled."

Hunter's family continued to believe that he did not abuse Tracey.

"He did not have an abusive, an angry bone in his body," Hunter's aunt Gina said. "In fact, we kind of laughed at him because he was too laid-back."

The divorce was finalized in October of 2010.

EVIDENCE OF ABUSE?

Loran Richards was the first of Tracey's friends to notice the minor injuries on her body. She would inquire about the bruises but the answers she received were always evasive. Seeing Tracey with a black eye, however, forced her to try and get more answers.

"I said, Tracey, you may have terrible luck," Richards recalled. "But nobody is so unlucky that they trip, fall down the stairs, and hit their face on a baseball in the eye socket. So don't give me a lame excuse. You don't have to give me any excuse, but let's take a picture."

Tracey broke down. She gave her friend all of the grisly details, detailing the abuse she suffered at the hands of Hunter. Loran then became her advocate, taking pictures of Tracey's injuries. She would later state that she saw blood stains and other signs of abuse at Tracey's home.

THAT FATEFUL NIGHT

Now divorced, Hunter would arrive at Tracey's home on November 22nd, 2010.

According to Tracey, he then became enraged when Tracey told him that she had spent the night with a new lover.

"He told me that he was gonna kill me," Tracey recalled. Tracey stated that she tried to escape, running into the closet in order to "get away from the kids and to pray." Tracey's eleven-year-old son from a previous relationship was in the home as was the four-year-old daughter they have together.

Hunter caught up with her and knocked her to the ground. He tied a belt around her ankles and then began choking her.

Half-conscious, Tracey alleged to have been raped and sodomized.

The brutal attack would leave Tracey unconscious. She would wake up the next morning on the bathroom floor.

"I called Hunter," Tracey recalled. "I told him that I was bleeding and that I was hurt and that I needed help. And he told me, 'Fuck you. I hope you die.'"

Tracey wound up in the emergency room after the attack. Hospital records would show that she had a laceration on her head, bruises, and ligature marks on her feet.

Tracey would then be referred to the Turning Point domestic violence center.

Marian Waters would describe Tracey's injuries as among the worst she had ever seen in a twenty-year career.

Waters would testify that Tracey had suffered a horrific assault. She described her mental state as typical of someone who had just been raped; fearful, jumpy, fearing for her life.

Tracey had suffered a hematoma on her side that was the side of a grapefruit. She also claimed to have experienced rectal nerve damage which would require surgery as well as torn vaginal muscles requiring her to have a hysterectomy.

Police were called and Hunter would be arrested for rape, sodomy, kidnapping and domestic violence.

"And at that point, I feared for my life," Tracey recalled. "And I feared for my children's life."

A HIDDEN AGENDA

Hunter would be freed on bail but Tracey got a restraining order against him. She bought a gun and did not go anywhere unarmed.

She took photos of her injuries on the night of the alleged attack and texted them to Loran. Later, they would take more pictures.

Angered, Hunter would stop paying her spousal and child support. Tracey, however, may have had another scenario in mind for obtaining money.

She had forced Hunter to take out a $103,000 life insurance policy around the time their daughter was born.

On May 24, 2012, the day before Tracey shot Hunter, she would place a call to MetLife that was recorded.

"Thank you for calling MetLife, this is Pam. May I please have your name?"

"Tracey Grissom."

Tracey would then explain that she was angry that her husband stopped making payments on his policy. During their divorce proceedings, he had agreed to continue paying the premiums. Tracey stated she was calling to make sure that they had the correct address on file.

"Is there anything else I can do for you today?

"That's gonna be it!" Tracey said, hanging up.

"Well, May 14th was just like any other day," Tracey said, explaining the call to the insurance company. "However, I had moved four different times. Me and my children were running. We were running from Hunter. So I had called the company to let them know that they had my old address and to make an address change."

FALSE RAPE?

Shelly Standridge was hired by Hunter to defend him in the rape case. She would state that Hunter denied raping or even assaulting Tracey that night. Hunter did, however, admit to the fact that he and his wife had consensual sex that night...Rough consensual sex.

"So that night," Standridge said. "Hunter said that she was depressed and claiming she was going to kill herself. She was saying she wanted their relationship to work."

So she undressed in front of him. Her beauty was always impossible for Hunter to resist.

The two had sex despite Hunter having a new girlfriend at home.

Hunter's aunt, Gina, believed that Tracey wanted to kill Hunter before the rape case went to court.

"He had a new girlfriend, he was living with her," Phelps said. "He was moving on with his life. Hunter would claim that Tracey was jealous, obsessive, even stalked them."

"Hunter had moved on," Hunter's aunt said. "There was some court dates coming up that would prove that Hunter was innocent. There were court dates coming up that he would get visitation to his daughter. She had a lot to lose."

Tracey was on the anti-anxiety drug Klonopin. Hunter would tell his attorney that Tracey would take more than her prescribed dose. Because of this, she fell and cut her head. Hunter would then leave the house around 10:30 pm and go to his father's house. Tracey would call him hours later, at 3:20 am.

Hunter would state that Tracey had called to threaten him. She told him if he didn't want the responsibility of the children then she would make it where he would never be able to see them again.

Hunter's attorney did not know what Tracey's motive was for crying rape. She was very upset that he had a girlfriend.

MORE LIES...

Hunter would be arrested nearly twelve hours later, to his total shock.

Tracey would give her side of the story to the police which later is proven to be false.

She would tell police that Hunter had thrown her against the bathtub around 10 pm and claim to be unconscious until 4 am the next morning.

"But her phone records show she was on the phone all night, so she was never unconscious," Standridge said. "She was also using her data at 10:42 that night. She was using it again at 10:50 that night. ... She sends a text to her boyfriend at 1:49 am. She sends a text to her friend at 2:07 am. She sends another text to her boyfriend at 2:07 am."

Tracey would blame the calls on Hunter.

"All I do know is I was not the only person using my phone that night," Tracey said, suggesting that Hunter used her phone.

Medical records would show that Tracey's head wound was "purely superficial".

Only one suture was needed.

Furthermore, there was nothing on the medical record to support the fact that Tracey experienced vaginal and rectal tears. She did have bruises on her ankle and legs but the photos taken by police at the emergency room would not resemble the same photos that Tracey and her friend Loran would take days later. In the photos taken at the emergency room, an area of Tracey's body has no bruises. Days later, there is discoloration.

Tracey's attorney would blame the discrepancy on "blood thinners" which would cause Tracey to bruise easily.

There was also a discrepancy in her phone records. She would take a photo of her inner thigh, a deep bruise. This area of her body was not photographed by police during her emergency room visit. But on December 9th, almost two weeks later, Tracey took a photo of her inner thigh with the deep bruise

"He (Hunter) told me that he would make it to where nobody would ever want me," Tracey said after a 2010 attack. "I didn't report it because I thought he would kill me."

THE FINAL STRAW

Tracey woke up pissed on May 15th, 2012.

Hunter had been ordered to pay $2,100 a month for the rest of his life. He was not complying with the court order claiming that he was "out of work."

Tracey stated that she was on her way to a job interview when she saw a Grissom Construction sign out of the corner of her eye.

She stated that her initial plan was to take a photograph of Hunter at the job site in order to show proof that he was working as part of her litigation.

"I was getting ready to take the picture and when I looked up he was standing almost directly towards the front of the boat trailer," Tracey said. "He was looking back directly at me. He had this face, that's like mean - just, I don't know how to describe it. I mean, I see it over and over like it's right there all the time. He flipped me the bird, which to me was kinda like, 'Yeah I'm workin. Screw you.' And at that point, I panicked. At that point, I didn't know what else to do except to defend myself."

Tracey started firing. The first shot hit Hunter in the arm. He started to run and she fired again repeatedly. One of the bullets punctured Hunter's heart and he died of massive internal bleeding.

William Dockery was working with Hunter and was an eyewitness to the shooting. Hunter had turned to Dockery before the shooting and told him to "call the law". Before Dockery could pick up his cell phone, Tracey had commenced shooting.

Tracey then pulled out her own cell phone and called the cops on herself. She tearfully described that she had just murdered her husband.

CONFESSION

Tracey told detectives exactly what was going through her mind when she came upon Hunter at the construction site.

"Tell me about what happened," the detective said. "What led up to...what's going on."

"In November of 2010, he beat me unconscious and raped me...and, and left me for dead....and, and I finally pressed charges against him and he told me that he would make my life a living hell...and that's what he's done."

"What, what happened this morning that led up to you going..."

"I was going to work and I saw him...and he's been claiming that he-he's not working. And, so I pulled in there to take a picture of him...cause it was the truck that's still in my name...and the boat that's still in my name...and the trailer that's still in my name...He just stared at me and flipped me off...and I just went in there and shot him...I just shot him, I shot him, and I shot him."

Tracey would be distraught and tearful during her interrogation room confession. A few weeks later, however, she would call the insurance company to let them know that Hunter had died.

"Well, I was actually calling because I didn't know what I needed to do ... Hunter passed away May 15th and I actually am going a court case right now because it was due to self-defense..."

Hunter's family went ballistic over this. Tracey would claim that she had no money but she continued to pay his life insurance premiums.

"Even through the times when she's screamin' that she's destitute and has no money ... she continued to pay life insurance premium," Hunter's mother said.

"I don't think my sister concocted a story," Tracey's sister said. "Just so she could get insurance money. ... But that's all they (the prosecution) had."

THE TRIAL

Tracey's allegations of rape and sodomy would not be allowed in court testimony. She was allowed, however, to detail the effects of Hunter's abuse on her were.

Taking the stand, Tracey would lift up her shirt in court and show herself wearing a colostomy bag. She stated that she had undergone several surgeries after her husband's daily rapes wherein she suffered permanent rectal and vaginal damage.

Hunter's family was then allowed to speak at the hearing.

"This tremendous loss has changed me," Hunter's mother, Melanie Garner said. "And I don't know how to change back."

Chloe, Hunter's sister, had a victim's services officer read her letter in court.

"Tracey is psychotic," Chloe wrote. "She is the most selfish person human being on this earth."

"Every mother should pray every night that your son doesn't fall in love with someone like Tracey," Hunter's aunt, Gina Grissom said. "There have been lots of allegations against Hunter. We've never believed anything that has come out of her (Tracey's) mouth."

His aunt then looked directly at Tracey.

"Hunter was proud of his name. Why would you still choose to use our name, and bring it down?" suggesting that if Tracey hated him so much why didn't she go revert to her maiden name after the divorce.

The jurors would find Tracey guilty of murder. She would be sentenced to twenty-five years in prison.

One of the jurors, Janice Kelly, would contact Grissom's attorney Warren Freeman the morning after the trial. She had remorse over her decision and said that she wouldn't have convicted her had they had the rapes and abuse allegations been introduced as evidence.

"I feel I made a mistake," Kelly said. "If I had to do it over again, we'd have had a hung jury. We didn't get her side. She did not get a fair trial."

"We voted to convict because there was no dispute that Tracey shot Hunter," the jury foreman wrote in a letter that was addressed in the courthouse. "Jurors didn't believe prosecutor claims that she did it in order to collect a life insurance policy. We felt the shooting was a crime of passion, not for financial gain and that she should be sentenced accordingly. I wish we had seen evidence of the rape allegation. We feel that she just 'lost it.'"

"It's not fair, it's not fair!" Tracey sobbed as she was led out of the courthouse and to jail.

"We think the sentencing was too harsh," Tracey's attorney Warren Freeman said. "Considering you have the foreperson of the jury actually saying, we don't feel like she should be punished according to being found guilty of murder. Let's just say that there will be a basis for a new trial, and part of it will be something that the jurors saw that they weren't supposed to see and I'm going to just leave it at that until I file my motion."

"My son died running for his life," Hunter's mother said. "I don't know what was running through his mind but I hear him say 'momma.'"

"People who think that I murdered him in cold blood," Tracey said. "Either don't know the whole story or don't know everything that's happened.

Tracey was asked on CBS' 48 hours if she regretted pulling the trigger on that fateful day.

"No," she said flatly. "Because if I hadn't I would be dead. I truly believe that."

"She has a way of making everything she does look right," Hunter's aunt, Gina scoffed.

HUSBAND KILLER : THE TRUE STORY OF KELLY GISSENDANER

42

JENNIFER KENDALL

Kelly Gissendaner, born Kelly Brookshire, became the sixth and last woman executed in Georgia for her role in the murder of her husband, Douglas Gissendaner, by her lover, Greg Owen. The murder was gruesome, Kelly demonstrated a lack of credibility with lies, and the murder was clearly premeditated- three things that helped a jury convict her of her role in the murder. What hurt her the most, though, was that her former lover turned on her and testified against her. Kelly seemingly changed her life in prison, mentoring and preaching to other women. Her legal team appealed the decision due to a lack of proof, her redemption, and her relationship with her children. The mother of three children cried and sang "Amazing Grace" as she received the lethal injection and one hundred people protested her death outside.

Early Life

In 1968, Kelly Brookshire was born to Maxine and Marry Brookshire in Georgia. She has a brother that was born one year after Kelly. Kelly and her brother were not born into wealth or emotional stability. Her family consisted of simple cotton farmers. Her parents drank, did drugs, and fought. Due to the troubled relationship, they did not stay together. Kelly's father left the family and created a new one with no intention of including Kelly into his new family dynamic. This obviously left Kelly feeling unwanted and abandoned. Kelly's mother did remarry a man named Billy Wade eight days after the divorce with Kelly's father was final, but Billy only added more trauma to Kelly's already broken home. Many people came forward with knowledge of sexual abuse to Kelly by her stepfather and other men. On top of the sexual abuse, Billy Wade was physically and emotionally abusive to Kelly, her brother, and her mother. Luckily, her mother also divorced Billy Wade and moved the family.

Kelly stood at six feet tall, and she was rather homely looking. Many people made fun of her for her looks and being "trailer trash". She would prefer to work rather than socialize, mostly due to her household's financial situation and her mother's strict rules. Her first job was at McDonald's. She mostly kept to herself, but the outcast made one friend in a woman named Mitzi.

First child and marriage

Kelly got pregnant with her first child before she finished high school. She claimed that the child was conceived through date rape, and the father was not actively involved in the child's life. She refused to name the father to even her best friends. She also tried to hide the pregnancy for as long as she could, but the reality became apparent around her sixth month. Before she gave birth, her father reached out to her and suggested that she name the child with his last name. Her first child, Brandon Brookshire, was born in June of 1986. Kelly married her first husband, Jeff Banks, at the young age of nineteen, but the marriage only lasted for six months before it dissolved. Reports indicate that the marriage quickly ended when Kelly's father threatened Jeff with a gun for not passing him bread at the dinner table. After the marriage ended, Kelly and her baby moved into her mother's trailer. This was a rough time for Kelly, but she was saved when she met Douglas Gissendaner.

Marriage to Douglas Gissendaner

On September 2, 1989, Kelly became Mrs. Douglas Gissendaner... for the first time. Kelly was four months pregnant on her wedding day, which could have encouraged the nuptials. The marriage was tumultuous from the beginning. They had financial difficulty after they both lost their jobs and were forced to live with Doug's parents for some time. However, Doug provided a good life for Kelly and her child when he decided to enlist in the United States Army. Despite a steady paycheck, Kelly used the money irresponsibly and needed Doug's family to help her with car payments. Doug's parents already didn't love Kelly, and this added to their distrust. When Doug moved to Germany because of his job in the army, it only added to the tension. The move happened only one month after Kelly had given birth to their first child together and her second child, Kayla. When Kelly and Doug were together, they were noticeably miserable. The relationship did not work at all, and they fought constantly. People also spoke up about Kelly's partying and sleeping around with other men while Doug wasn't around. This caused even more strain on the family, and the couple divorced in 1993. This time, Kelly joined the army with no other way to support herself and her children, but she discovered that she was not made for the army. During this time, Kelly became pregnant with another man and gave birth to her final child Jonathan who everyone called Cody. This father would die of cancer shortly after his birth. After returning from the army, Kelly and Doug reconciled. Despite having a child with another man, they didn't want to separate their family. They remarried in May of 1995 and, despite a separation during this time, bought a house together in Auburn, Georgia in December of 1996. A few months later, Doug was murdered.

Greg Owen

While divorced from Doug, Kelly started working for the International Readers League of Atlanta. At this time, she started socializing with her boss, Belinda Owens. When she met Belinda's brother Greg Owen, they had an instant chemistry. The relationship started strong, but it soon started to worry Belinda. Belinda noticed an alarming amount of fighting, and she didn't appreciate the bossy tone that Kelly used when she spoke to her brother. Kelly and Greg broke up, and Kelly went back to Doug and remarried. Kelly and Greg rekindled their romance during a brief separation between Kelly and Douglas, but Kelly ultimately stayed married to Douglas. Many suspect her devotion to her relationship with Doug involved stability for her and her children rather than love. This was only amplified by the fact that many reports indicated that she continued to maintain a relationship with Owen throughout her marriage to Douglas.

Murder and Investigation

In February 7, 1997, Douglas Gissendaner was murdered by in a secluded part of rural Gwinnett County. Douglas came home from a friend's house shocked to find Gregory Owen in his home. Gregory then exhibited a knife and forced Douglas to drive to a remote area. When they stopped, Owen forced Douglas out of the car and made him walk 300 feet into the woods before beating him in the skull with a nightstick and repeatedly stabbing him in the neck and back. When Kelly arrived, she helped set the car on fire to eliminate any evidence.

The night of the murder, Kelly had gone out for dinner and drinks with friends. Despite dancing and having a good time, she went home right around midnight. Friends with her that night reported that she told them that she went home because she had a feeling that there was something wrong. Kelly frantically searched for Doug when he didn't come home the next day. She made several calls, but she reportedly could not locate him. She even called his parents to ask if they had seen him. That same day a missing person's report was created by the local police department, and they started their search immediately.

Investigators had trouble with Kelly's story from the start. When she spoke with them, she described her marriage as happy and noneventful, but other people provided reports of fighting and numerous problems including Kelly's infidelity. One name that came up over and over again in interviews with friends and family was Greg Owen.

Greg Owen seemed to have a reasonable alibi. A roommate stated that he was home all night and got picked up by a friend for work the following morning at 9:00 a.m. With his roommate's alibi, police put Greg's interrogation on hold and continued their investigation.

Investigators finally got a big clue when they found Doug's car. It was left on a rural road in Gwinnett County. The most interesting thing about finding the car was that it appeared to be burned from the inside. At this time, there was no sign of Doug. While the situation didn't look good for Doug, family and friends knew that police were getting closer to the truth.

The day that the car was found, friends and family gathered to the home of Doug Sr. and Sue Gissendaner to support them during this difficult time. Kelly made an appearance, but she didn't stay long. She decided instead to take her children to the circus. While some people can understand how the environment can be traumatic to the children and maybe Kelly wanted to protect them, people found her decision evasive and questionable. Also, shouldn't the children be allowed to mourn with their grandparents? To increase suspicion even more, Kelly went back to work only four days into the search for her missing husband. Her behavior confused people around her. Sure, she had bills to pay, but four days was very soon to go back to work. Many people thought that she was hiding something. Many more people reported a weird attitude for a woman who had a missing husband.

After an already excruciating twelve days for Doug's friends and family, Doug's body was finally found in a horrific condition a mile from where they had found his car. His body appeared to be a bag of trash at first. He was on his knees, bent over, with his face in the dirt. Twelve days of decomposition, the elements, and animal attacks made him virtually unrecognizable. Medical professionals used dental records to confirm that the body was indeed Doug Gissendaner. He had been stabbed four times in the head, neck, and back.

While there was a long list of potential suspects, investigators kept Kelly close. When they talked to her again to go over her initial statements, the pressure must have gotten to her. She finally admitted that she had spoken to Greg on occasion when he called her. She made it clear to police that she did not pursue any relationship with Greg, and he pursued her. She also admitted that she reconciled with Owen during a separation, and she told investigators that he said that he would kill Doug when he found that she was getting back together with him. At this time, she pointed the finger at Greg and police questioned him heavily. Their relationship was officially over.

With the investigation focused on Greg, Greg's roommate changed his story completely. He was afraid that his leis could get him in trouble, and he told the police a new story. In fact, he confessed to investigators that Greg had been gone the night before until 8 am the next morning. With Greg's alibi gone, investigators knew they were getting even closer to the truth.

Kelly's story was raveling apart as well when investigators pulled up phone records that showed 47 calls between the two. They also saw that Kelly initiated the calls 18 times, which goes against what she told them while interrogated that she only spoke to him because he constantly called her. Furthermore, the correspondence ended immediately after the murder. Why would they stop talking so suddenly for no reason? Her inconsistencies made her look bad to the investigators who were suspicious of her story from the beginning.

After more interrogation, Greg confessed to the murder after he was told that cooperation could prevent him from getting the death penalty. He proceeds to implicate Kelly to save himself. He explains how he and Kelly had an intimate relationship, and she told Greg that she wanted him to kill Doug after they settled into their new house. She even came up with alibis at this time. He goes on to describe the murder in detail. He stated that Kelly picked him up and allowed her into his house. She even gave him the nightstick and the knife that he would use to attack her husband. She advised him to make it look like a home invasion and robbery. Greg waited until Doug got home at around 11 pm, and then he forced him to drive out to the boondocks by knifepoint. They eventually stopped, and Greg forced Doug out of the car and told him to walk. He committed the horrible murder by hitting him in the head with the nightstick and then stabbing him repeatedly, leaving him to bleed. Once completed, Kelly arrived with kerosene to get rid of the evidence. After the murder, Kelly told Greg that they shouldn't speak anymore until things die down. This is the confession that Greg gave police. With this confession, Greg only received a sentence of twenty five years to life instead of the death penalty.

As soon as the police had Greg's confession, they went to also arrest Kelly. They barged into her home on February 25th and completed the arrest. Kelly changed her story once again after her arrest. She confessed that she saw Greg Owen the night of the murder. This time she said that he called her, and she went to pick him up. When he picked her up, he told her about the murder. He then proceeded to threated to murder her and her children as well if she did not help him. Even though the police didn't believe her, Kelly maintained her innocence. Greg was only lying to save himself! She even turned down the plea deal offered to her and decided to go to trial. It was the same plea deal that the prosecution gave Greg- a guilty plea would give her twenty five to life, but she would not get the death penalty. Even her lawyer suggested that she take the plea deal, but Kelly decided to go to trial.

Trial

The first day of Kelly's trial was on November 2, 1998. The jury consisted of two men and ten women. Reporters were prevalent throughout the proceedings.

Prosecutors started by painting a picture of a troubled marriage between Kelly and Doug and her affair with Greg Owen. They then claimed that Gissendaner killed her husband to receive the house he bought for the family and two $10,000 life insurance policies. The reward was surprisingly small but substantial enough to be considered a motive alongside her affair. Prosecution also pointed out inconsistencies in her police reports of the night and the fact that Kelly specifically waited until Doug had bought the house for her and her children. She even had the foresight to plan alibis. This indicated that the murder was premeditated.

The prosecution brought many people into court to testify against Kelly. She faced her late husband's father, who was a witness in her trial. He brought up the troubled marriage between Kelly and his murdered son as well as her questionable relationship with Greg. While many people tried to argue that Doug Sr. already disliked Kelly, his closeness to the situation proved effective.

Another witness was Laura McDuffie. Laura McDuffie was an inmate who was in jail with Kelly. While the defense pointed out that the convict may not be the most trustworthy source and McDuffie only wanted time off of her sentence, her claims were convincing. McDuffie confessed that Kelly offered her $10,000 to take the fall for the murder of Doug Gissendaner. Kelly went so far as to provide a map and a handwritten statement of what McDuffie should say. A handwriting expert confirmed that the statement was in fact written by Kelly.

Kelly's own friend Pam was a witness for the prosecution, too. Pam told the jury that Kelly called her and told her that she had killed Doug. She called back at a later time and said that Greg had forced her to do it by threatening to kill her and her children. Pam claimed that Kelly said, "I did it,", but the defense claimed that pam heard incorrectly. Other friends also stepped up to voice they're uneasiness with her behavior while her husband was missing.

The strongest witness for the prosecution, though, was Greg Owen. His statement matched very closely with his confession, but there were certain differences that poked holes in his statement. He originally said that he drove for some time and then Kelly arrived when Doug was dead. He changed the time that Kelly showed up to the murder scene as he was finishing murdering Doug. Doug originally stated that he and Kelly burned the car together, but he then changed his story to say that Kelly simply threw a bottle of kerosene out of the window for him and he burned the car alone. Even with some holes in his original story, the confession remained very damning for Kelly. The former lovers found themselves implicating each other in their once common scheme.

The defense stated that the prosecution could not prove Kelly's innocence beyond a reasonable doubt. Furthermore, Doug Gissendaner was significantly larger than Greg and was also trained by the military. It seemed unreasonable that Doug would obey Greg's commands even if he did have a knife. Greg showed no sign of injury or struggle. It also didn't seem fair that Greg only got a life sentence when he was the one who committed the murder. Also, Greg's testimony, which was part of a plea bargain, gave him incentive to implicate Kelly for a lower sentence for himself.

In the end, a trial of her peers found Kelly Gissendaner guilty after deliberating for only two hours and sentenced her to the death penalty. In just a couple of words, Kelly's life came to an end. However, she was going to do whatever she could to save herself.

Life in Prison

Kelly was taken to prison where she was the only woman on death row. Being on death row, Kelly did her best to retain a relationship with her three children. She also continued to appeal her case, focus on her spiritual health, and mentor other prisoners.

While on death row, Kelly could not socialize with the general prison population. However, she could preach and act as a spiritual guide by talking to inmates through a vent. Mrs. Gissendaner created a bit of a name for herself in prison, and the women inmates supported her throughout her trial. They even called themselves the Struggle Sisters and rallied for her to be taken off of death row and allowed to live the rest of her life in prison.

Execution Reschedules

Her actual execution was actually the third time that Gissendaner had been scheduled for execution. She was previously scheduled for execution at the end of February, but the date was changed due to complications with winter weather. Next, she was scheduled for execution in the first week of March, but the doctors at the prison were concerned because the drug used to perform the lethal injection appeared cloudy. They sent a specimen to be tested, and, in April, they announced the results that there was nothing wrong. Gissenander's lawyers tried claiming that the changes in her execution date constituted cruel and unusual treatment, but the case was thrown out. If anything, Kelly was given more time, but her lawyers fought to the end.

Death

It was 12:21 a.m. on a Wednesday morning in Jackson, Georgia when officials declared Kelly MN Gissendaner dead from lethal injection. Her execution was scheduled for 7:00 p.m., but her lawyers attempted to repeal the decision to the very end. One hundred people stood outside of the Georgia Diagnostic and Classification Center in protest of her death. Her last meal was nachos, chips with cheese dip, and frozen lemonade.

Gissendaner showed remorse for her part in her ex-husband's death until the very end. Her last words were, "Bless you all. Tell the Gissendaners I am so, so sorry that an amazing man lost his life because of me. If I could take it all back, I would." Her words can be interpreted to indicate a sense of guilt on Gissendaner's part. It can also be interpreted to indicate a peace with her position.

Kelly Gissendaner was the only woman at death row for the entire duration of her time incarcerated, and she was the first woman to be given the death penalty in Georgia since 1945- over 70 years. She was one of only six women executed in the state, and she was the last woman to be executed in Georgia.

Appeals and Support

Kelly's lawyers made a valiant attempt at an appeal. In fact, the appeal was more than fifty pages when they turned it in, and it had statements from a number of different people, including inmates, the pope, and political figures.

After being approached by Mrs. Gissendaner's lawyer, the pope responded in a letter stating, "While not wishing to minimize the gravity of the crime for which Ms. Gissendaner has been convicted, and while sympathizing with the victims, I nonetheless implore you, in consideration of the reasons that have been presented to your Board, to commute the sentence to one that would better express both justice and mercy."

The endorsement by the pope was powerful, but the Catholic Church had also just recently vocalized a stance against the death penalty. Even former Georgia Supreme Court Chief Justice Norman Fletcher stood up for the defendant saying that her role in the murder did not constitute the death penalty. In addition to these endorsements, 90,000 people also signed a petition to support Kelly. Kelly's lawyers showed the courts that Kelly showed remorse and represented a criminal who had turned her life around to bring positivity to those around her. They argued that her presence was significantly greater than her absence to those around her, especially her children and other inmates.

Mrs. Gissendaner's lawyers attempted three appeals to the U.S. Supreme Court, but they were denied all three times. Unfortunately, on the day of the execution, Mrs. Gissendaner's children had to choose between saying good-bye to their mother or appearing in front of a judge for one last attempt to appeal her case. The last time that they saw their mother was two days earlier on Monday. In the most heartbreaking of all testimonies, Kelly's daughter, Kayla pleaded with the court to save her mother's life. She made the point that she had already lost her dad, and he would not want her or her siblings to endure any further loss by also losing their mother. Despite the emotional appear and strong endorsements, the court did not waver on its original decision.

Despite the support from multiple sources, Douglas's family, especially his father, maintained throughout the trial that they trusted the legal system and agreed with the sentence of the death penalty. They reminded the public that she chose to go to trial instead of pleading guilty. They also reminded the public that Douglas did not get any choice in what happened to his life. After the gruesome death of their son, an exhausting and emotional search for the truth, and a prolonged trial, Douglas Gissendaner Sr. and Sue Gissendaner got justice.

Death Penalty Debate

Kelly Gissendaner's case became famous across the nation because of its legal implications regarding the death penalty. People for the death penalty noted that Kelly had orchestrated the entire murder, she helped dispose of the body, she lied multiple times, and the family of Douglas Gissendaner deserved justice. People opposed to the death penalty noted that there was room for doubt, she technically did not commit the murder, the person who did commit the murder escaped the death penalty, she showed remorse over her part in the murder, she experienced trauma in her childhood, and she regularly preached and encouraged other women in the prison. Men and women all over the country debated the case, but, ultimately, the death penalty ruling was honored by the state of Georgia, and Kelly was executed while she sobbed and sang "Amazing Grace". She was 47-years-old.

WENDI ANDRIANO

Chapter 1

A dying husband needs a devoted wife. But when love runs out, marriage becomes a burden.

On October 8, 2000, Wendi Andriano snapped. She had played the part of devoted wife to her terminally ill husband, Joe Andriano, for years, but when the love left their marriage, so did Wendi's patience for her husband's eventual demise.

Wendi had a plan to help nudge nature along, and when her plan b expired, she took matters directly into her own hands and bludgeoned him to death.

Wendi first tried to poison her husband by spiking his last meal, a homemade beef stew, with sodium azide, but Joe Andriano did not ingest enough to kill him, only enough to vomit it back up. Wendi then grabbed the nearest object, a bar stool, and beat her dying husband over the head so many times that parts of his brain became exposed.

After thinking she had successfully killed her husband twice, Wendi then realized that Joe was still breathing, so she took a knife from the family kitchen and stabbed him in the side of the throat.

Minutes later, Joe was finally dead.

This bizarre and frantic way Wendi killed her husband isn't the strangest thing about the case though. Known even to Wendi, Joe was due to die from terminal cancer within the next few years anyways.

Why Wendi couldn't wait to kill her husband is an intriguing tale wrought with sex, lies, and strangely, a lack of patience.

Chapter 2

Wendi and Joe Andriano grew up together in the small farming community of Casa Grande, Arizona. But while they both had gone to the same school, they never dated. As a minister's daughter, Wendi's social life was restricted to her father's church. Her celebration for graduating high school was even in the form of a missionary trip to

Mexico in 1989. When she returned she took a job at the local clerical hospital.

Wendi met Joe in 1992 through friends. Although when the couple started dating Joe's family found the minister's daughter to be an unusual fit for the loud, outgoing former football player, they all thought she was friendly enough and approved of the match.

Joe worked for a local boat builder. He was very mechanically inclined and was a very good welder. He owned his own boat and took Wendi for several cruises around the local hot spots for speedboats. They were inseparable.

The couple married in January of 1994. Their wedding took place in a baptist church across the street from their shared elementary school. Their reception was at the Elk's club and was populated by their many friends and family. Even after two years of dating, though, Joe's family felt like they didn't know his new bride very well, but Joe seemed to be very happy, so they were happy for him.

Soon after marrying, the couple became business partners when they started a small company that did windshield repair and replacement. The business combined Wendi's office experience with Joe's mechanical experience, skills they both exceeded at, and the business thrived.

The couple hadn't been married a whole year yet before they faced their first major challenge together. That fall, Joe noticed an odd bump on his neck. When he had it tested, he was told it was a non-cancerous benign tumor, but it wasn't long before they were second-guessing the diagnoses. A year after it was removed, the tumor grew back.

A second surgery and round of tests seemed to reconfirm that the tumor was benign, but shortly after Wendi gave birth to a son in 1997, the tumor was back yet again.

The third time the tumor returned, Joe's wife and family were convinced that the tumor had to be cancer. This fear was confirmed in 1998 when Joe underwent surgery to have the bump removed for the fourth time. Joe's pre-surgery chest x-ray showed that not only was the tumor cancerous, but that the cancer had now spread across Joe's throat, chest, and lungs.

The prognosis wasn't good—Joe had a rare form of cancer and while radiation and chemotherapy were standard, there was no guarantee they would work. On top of this, Wendi was also pregnant again and was only months away from giving birth to the couple's second child.

Chapter 3

In an effort to increase Joe's chances of survival while decreasing his suffering, Wendi and Joe decided to pursue holistic treatments before resorting to chemotherapy and radiation. They had been told that chemotherapy and radiation treatments would likely not cure Joe, but they would lengthen his life by a few years; however, these years would be anything from pleasant. The horrific side-effects chemotherapy and radiation treatments cause are well known.

So the Andriano's decided first to try anything from special diets to alternative medical treatments to prayer—anything that had a chance to help Joe. Joe even attended a holistic treatment centre for cancer patients in Colorado for a few weeks where he was surrounded by other men and women facing the same prognosis as him. After seeing the bravery of others in the same position as him, Joe began thinking about his future again and began to see it as bright for the first time in a while.

After Joe returned from his holistic healing getaway with a bright new attitude, the Andriano's decided the next best step would be for Joe to begin chemotherapy treatments. He had begun to crave his future and was ready to take steps to achieve it. Unfortunately, taking these steps meant that Joe needed to quit his welding job as well as his own position in the couple's business.

To help make ends meet, Wendi returned to working for the first time since the birth of the couple's children. She ended up taking multiple jobs and worked long hours while continuing to care for her husband at home. Eventually, Wendi landed a job managing the San Riva apartment complex in the Ahwatukee foothills, an upscale neighbourhood outside of Phoenix.

Wendi's new job came with some major perks—the salary was above average, which was nice as Wendi was now the family's breadwinner, and it required Wendi to live on site, which meant that the family now lived in a luxury apartment but paid no rent. Wendi's new job also gave her a new life. A large part of her duties as complex manager was arranging social activities for the other residents of the San Riva apartments, who were mostly young, wealthy, single businesspeople.

Every Saturday the complex hosted picnics, pool parties, or late-night socials. The residents even had their own baseball team. Wendi was required to attend every event, which meant Joe was needed to stay home with their two children. Wendi enjoyed this alone time so much that many of the residents at the San Riva had no clue she had a dying husband and two children at home. She partied like she was single.

The first few months at the San Riva went well. Wendi organized mixers and pool parties for the tenants while Joe took care of the kids. Despite being very weak from treatments, he did everything he could, he wanted to do it. He prefered to have his kids around him even when he didn't feel good.

Although they had never gotten close to their daughter-in-law, Joe's parents also pitched in with babysitting so the couple could have time alone together. They didn't get to see each other much as Wendi began spending more and more time at work. Her new job had also given her a new confidence, and she spent many nights out on the town dancing and drinking away her weekday stress with friends. Joe began to fear that Wendi would soon leave him for her new lifestyle, but this fear got sidetracked when his health continued to fail.

In the summer of 2000, when tests revealed his cancer had spread yet again, Joe and Wendi decided to increase the frequency of Joe's chemotherapy. Joe agreed to undergo more treatments, but they quickly took their toll. He lost 15 pounds in the first week alone, and Joe's doctor became concerned. It went from bad to worse very quickly.

By the beginning of October 2000, it became harder and harder to remain optimistic about Joe's chances of beating his cancer. It became apparent it was terminal, but doctors insisted that with treatment Joe could live for several more years.

No one had any idea that Joe would be dead after only the first week of the month. No one, that is, except for one person—Wendi Andriano.

Chapter 4

Just after 2:00 a.m. on October 8, Wendi Andriano called a friend who also lived in the San Riva apartment complex. She told her friend that she needed someone to stay with the kids while she took Joe to the hospital. When the friend arrived, she found Joe on the floor, barely alive.

Joe was on the floor in the fetal position. There was vomit on the floor around him and he couldn't stand up. Wendi confided in her friend that she told Joe that she had called 9-1-1 and paramedics were on the way, but this wasn't true. After seeing Joe in such poor condition, the neighbour urged Wendi to call paramedics. She then went outside to wait for them to arrive while Wendi waiting with her husband.

Wendi did call 9-1-1, but when the EMT's arrived minutes later, she refused to let them or her friend inside the apartment. She said that her husband was dying from terminal cancer and had a do not resuscitate order. Joe was not to receive any medical attention.

Just over an hour later, at 3:30 a.m., Wendi dialed 9-1-1 a second time. The same team of paramedics came to the house. It didn't take them long to realize something wasn't quite right, so they contacted the police department. Both the paramedics and the police were shocked to find out that Joe, who had been terminally ill from cancer for quite some time had died, but not from the cancer that had been slowly killing his body. He died from being repeatedly beaten with a bar stool and from being stabbed in the neck.

When the police opened the front door of the apartment, they were confronted with obvious signs of a deadly struggle. The apartment was in a complete state of disarray, and there was blood everywhere. Blood had been traced throughout the kitchen, the dining room, and the living room of the luxury apartment, and blood had spattered across the walls the ceilings. Lying in the middle of the bloody scene was Joe, with a knife wound in his neck and holes spattered across his visible skull.

While crime scene technicians surveyed the apartment, phoenix police took Wendi down to the station for a formal statement. She was wearing clothes drenched in Joe's blood and was armed with a story that explained how Joe's death had been a complete accident.

In the interrogation room, Wendi told police she and joe had spent the evening in Casa Grande visiting with Joe's parents. They put the kids to bed after they returned home, which was when Joe noticed something odd about Wendi's appearance—she wasn't wearing her wedding ring.

According to Wendi, Joe worked himself into a rage and began accusing her of having an affair. This argument turned into a shoving match, and when Joe grabbed a belt, Wendi grabbed a bar stool and swung. Joe went down on all fours so she hit him again. It was then that she called her neighbour for help. Joe may have been in a terrible state when the neighbour saw him, but according to Wendi when she went outside Joe had gotten back to his feet easily.

Wendi said she denied the EMTs access to the apartment because she and Joe were both embarrassed about the fight, but just minutes after the EMTs left, the fight got physical again.

Wendi said that her husband tried to strangle her with a telephone cord and she defended herself with the first weapon she could get in her hands—a kitchen knife. She was vague about how the knife ended up in Joe's neck though, saying she was holding the knife up when Joe suddenly fell flat on his face. The next thing she knew, blood was spurting everywhere. He must have fallen on the blade, it was simply an accident.

Many things about this story didn't make sense to the police. First of all, the timeline presented in Wendi's story didn't match the accounts of Wendi's neighbour or the EMTs. Wendi's neighbour had seen no evidence of a physical fight when they first entered the apartment—there were no broken bar stools or blood like later when the police arrived. As well, Wendi had few injuries on her body, definitely no injuries that would necessitate self defence in the form of murder.

Joe's illness also shed doubt on Wendi's story. Joe's parents told police that when the Andriano's visited earlier that evening, Joe had been so weak from his treatments that he could barely stand. They had spent the evening doting on their sick son, bringing him any comforts he wanted. If he was too weak to stand, he certainly couldn't have been strong enough to violently attack Wendi.

Police also uncovered a damning piece of evidence from Wendi herself, in a moment when she thought she was all alone. The investigators that had been questioning Wendi left her on her own in the interrogation room for some time while they fact checked some of her statements and checked in with the investigators who were scanning the crime scene for evidence. During this time, Wendi made a phone call to a coworker at the apartment complex and asked them to hide some of her files from the police. This immediately led to a search of Wendi's office where police found evidence that Wendi had in fact killed her husband. She had even been planning it for months.

Chapter 5

While both investigators strongly believed that Wendi Andriano was responsible for Joe's death, they were stumped by her motive. Why would Wendi kill her dying husband? The police didn't know, but they did have one intriguing lead—the phone call Wendi had made from the interrogation room. They were determined to find out what she was trying to hide.

When they searched her office, police discovered that Wendi had been disciplined at work for using her computer to search inappropriate items on the internet while on the clock.She had been conducting research on poisons, and how to use certain poisons to kill people. They also discovered the papers that she had tried to hide—shipping notices for a substance known as sodium azide.

Sodium azide is a lethal substance with a variety of industrial uses including propelling airbags. It is not, however, something that the average person can simply go out and buy. It's not restricted to the point where only certain companies can possess it, but it needs to be bought for a reason—something that an apartment complex didn't have. But based on the information on the shipping invoice, Wendi had found a way around that.

Wendi had created a fictitious business license using the tax ID form for the apartment complex. Using a Xerox machine and an exacto knife, Wendi had removed all information specific to the apartment complex and inserted fictitious information for a fake company.

The business name on the shipping notice was bogus, but the address wasn't. Wendi had the substance delivered to an address in Scottsdale, Arizona in an attempt to distance herself, but that plan didn't work. When the police tracked down the real address on the invoice, workers at the company positively identified Wendi as the person who had come by a couple weeks earlier to pick up a package she had mistakenly had shipped there instead of her own office.

Wendi's coworkers had seen her with a package but that she had been very mysterious with the contents. She refused to tell anyone what was inside. Had this been the sodium azide? And if so, where was it now?

Chapter 6

Suspecting that Wendi had tried to poison Joe with the sodium azide, police took samples of every medication and food they could find in the Andriano's apartment. If Joe had ingested poison, it would have explained the awful state Wendi's friend had seen him in just over an hour before he died. Luckily, the remainders of Joe's last supper, homemade beef stew, still sat in a pot on the stove.

However, police didn't find any evidence of Wendi's mysterious package, or any evidence of the sodium azide itself in Wendi and Joe's apartment. They had just begun to lose hope in finding the poison when they found out Wendi had a storage space in the building that she failed to tell the police about. Hidden behind a stack of boxes in Wendi's storage unit was a small bottle of white powder and a measuring spoon. The white powder was soon identified as sodium azide.

But the storage unit wasn't the only place investigators found the lethal substance—it was also in Joe's stomach contents and in the beef stew on the stove.

While discovering the poison helped police understand that Wendi had been trying to kill her husband, it didn't explain why she had bludgeoned him to death on October 8, 2000. Wendi had spent a lot of time researching poisons and she spent a lot of time manufacturing documents so that she could purchase the poison. It certainly wasn't a spur of the moment decision.

But why would Wendi beat and stab her husband if she had already poisoned him? Prosecutors had a theory, one that would cut to the heart of the crime. It was patience—or more precisely, Wendi's lack of it—that had killed Joe in the end.

Wendi had grown tired of waiting for the cancer to kill Joe, so she decided to give nature a little nudge by poisoning his supper. But according to the theory, when Wendi gave Joe the poison, things didn't go quite to plan. Joe hadn't ingested enough poison to kill him when he began vomiting it back up. With her plan quickly failing, Wendi panicked. She snapped.

Now improvising, Wendi beat Joe with the nearest object she could get her hands on—a bar stool. Pathologists were able to conclude that Wendi beat Joe over the head with the stool no less than twenty-four times. This beating did render Joe unconscious, but still didn't kill him so Wendi grabbed a kitchen knife and stabbed him in the part of his body that caused all this trouble in the first place—the side of his neck.

Chapter 7

Ten days after she murdered her husband, Wendi Andriano was formally charged with first degree murder. Wendi's crime was viewed as being especially cruel due to the large amount of suffering Joe had had to endure over several hours thanks to Wendi's actions. Because of this, the prosecutor's on Wendi's trial did the almost unthinkable, they sought the death penalty.

When Wendi a walked into the Arizona courtroom on September 9, 2004 she looked vastly different from the perky apartment manager that the residents of the San Riva apartments used to know.

At the time of the killing she had been blonde, she had short hair, and generally appeared to be much younger and cute than the individual who appeared in court with long dark hair and thick glasses. Previously, she had liked to look good and show her figure so her conservative dress at the trial was certainly different from the look her friends were used to seeing. She was trying to look more conservative, more innocent.

She had had plenty of time to perfect her new look—it had taken prosecutors almost four years to bring the case to trial. It had been postponed about 12 times before it was finally brought before a judge and jury.

In their opening statement, prosecutors reminded the jury that at the time of the murder Wendi had been anything but the perfect mother or wife she claimed to have been. She had been someone who had no disregard for her husband at all. While her husband was dying, she had gone out partying and started affairs, and when his condition worsened, and it began to cramp her style, she turned to poison.

Wendi didn't like her new role as family breadwinner, especially with the loss of Joe's income, and with rising medical bills, the family was in the worst financial state they had ever been in. Wendi had thought she was going to be able to be a stay-at-home-mom for the rest of her life, and she did not adjust well to her return to the workforce. So Wendi had found an out.

Although Joe did not have any life insurance, even though Wendi had asked several friends to pretend to be Joe in medical exams so he could be insured, Joe had filed a malpractice suit against his former doctor who had continually told him his tumor was benign when it was in fact spreading throughout his body. If Joe died and the lawsuit went through, Wendi would likely walk away with a multi-million dollar settlement.

More than money though, Wendi had wanted freedom. She wanted the freedom to be single again, she wanted freedom to the ball-and-chain who was slowly dragging her spirit into his grave along with himself. Wendi wanted to not have to care about her dying husband anymore, who was too weak to provide her with any love.

Wendi maintained her plea of innocence throughout the trial, and her defence team attempted to prove she had been the victim of abuse not only on the night of Joe's death but also throughout the couple's entire marriage. To explain the poison, Wendi told the court that Joe had been the one who had grown tired of waiting for the cancer to end his life, and had asked Wendi to help him do it himself.

On the witness stand Wendi said that Joe had willingly taken the poison, but she also stuck by the story that she had originally told police, that Joe had suspected an affair and became enraged when she affirmed them. He became deranged and attacked her, starting the bloody fight. Wendi claimed Joe had died during the ensuing struggle.

Wendi's story wasn't enough to convince the court though, and on November 18, 2004 she was found guilty of the crime. It had taken the jury only two-and-a-half-hours to come to its unanimous decision. Six years after her husband joe had been diagnosed with terminal cancer, Wendi Andriano faced a possible death sentence of her own.

On December 20, 2004, the jurors assigned to Wendi Andriano's case met and decided on Wendi's fate—it would be death for Ms Andriano. Wendi, along with most of the courtroom, was aghast. Even Joe's family was shocked by the decision. Wendi Andriano became the second ever woman to be put on death row in Arizona, a state that reserves the death penalty for the worst of the worst.

Wendi Andriano has since attempted to appeal the court's decision, but as of early 2017, all attempts have been denied and Wendi continues to wait on death row. Wendi and Joe's children now live with Joe's parents, who continue to mourn the loss of their beloved son.

Joe Andriano's death was especially long, and especially cruel, but no happy ending was found when Wendi was sentenced to her own death. Many view the conclusion of this case to be the saddest possible outcome. On October 8, 2000, two lives were lost, and two children were left without parents.

HUSBAND KILLER : THE TRUE STORY OF PAMELA PHILLIPS

67

ANITA ADONIS

Pamela Phillips, known as Pam, is currently serving life in jail for killing her ex-husband. But, is the former wealthy socialite really capable of murder? And why did it take almost 18 years for her to get caught?

Pam's early life was relatively unremarkable. She was born in 1958 to a wealthy family who had a rather frivolous lifestyle. Pam's father was short tempered and drank too much, whereas her mother was a calm and collected woman, who rarely showed any emotion. Perhaps, this combination gave Pam a steely edge and a hunger for the high life. For many years though, Pam seemed like a perfectly normal, ambitious woman. She was very beautiful and achieved a successful career as a real estate agent, growing to be worth between 1 and 2 million dollars.

Pam married young, but after a short time she divorced and became very involved in the Arizona social scene. It was in 1985, that she first laid eyes on Gary Triano. Triano was a successful businessman. He had earned his fortune investing in Native American Bingo halls. Triano was well known and well connected in Arizona. He had many wealthy friends, including Donald Trump. Pam was immediately attracted to Triano and his way of life. The pair began socialising regularly, often at parties held by Triano and his then wife, Mary Cram. Pam and Triano had an ongoing affair, which eventually resulted in Triano making the biggest mistake of his life. While Cram was abroad with the couple's two children, Heather and Brian, Triano messaged her to say that he was filing for divorce.

Less than a year later, Pam and Triano got married. The well off, attractive couple appeared to have it all; close friends described Triano as smitten. They married on a yacht in San Diego. The wedding was an extremely flashy, black-tie event, where guests could sample any drink imaginable.

The following years were dedicated to partying and travelling with other Arizona elites. Pam and Triano purchased a beautiful home in the poshest part of town. They also had two children together, Trevor and

Lois. Though Pam has since described Triano as abusive, obsessive and controlling, friends say that at the time she seemed very happy.

In the late 1980s, things started to go wrong. The financial fortunes of Tucson, Arizona, began to change. The real estate market crashed and many of Triano's investments failed. He quickly started developing some serious debts. In the early 1990s, Triano was dealt the biggest blow. The laws around gaming and Bingo halls changed, Native Americans were able to start claiming all the money earnt on the reservations, as their own. Triano was cut out. His earnings plummeted; losing as much as 93% of his income in one year. Triano was a man who borrowed from other individuals, rather than banks. Unable to pay his debts, Triano made quite a few enemies. In particular, a group of Northern Mexican investors that threatened to kill him if he filed for bankruptcy. A desperate Triano also made a dodgy deal with wealthy drug addict, Neil McNeice, another mobster who wanted to have Triano killed. All in all, Triano became a very unpopular guy. Despite various warnings, he filed for bankruptcy in 1994.

Pam was shocked. She had no idea about the true extent of Triano's financial problems. After he claimed bankruptcy however, everything began to come out. Pam learned of Triano's significant debts, totalling around $26 million, including owing his ex-wife $1.8 million and his attorney $97,000. Triano also had 74 pending lawsuits. The man was clearly in dire straits, and Pam was horrified. She had entered the marriage as a successful business woman, worth around 2 million dollars. But, during their time together, Pam had stopped working in order to raise the couple's two children. She later claimed that Triano pressured her to do this. She was about to be ruined. Pam stated that when Triano lost all his money, he became paranoid and extremely hard to live with. Whether or not this is true is extremely hard to say, maybe Pam just didn't want to be involved in Triano's embarrassing downfall. Either way, shortly after discovering the debts, Pam filed for divorce.

The divorce was finalised very quickly – in less than a month. Pam was awarded the house. Supposedly wanting to ditch her newly acquired bad reputation, Pam left Tucson. In an underhand move, she sold the marital house while Triano was away. She pocketed the $300,000 proceeds and in 1994, fled to Aspen with the couple's two children. Triano was left alone and in severe debt in Arizona.

In Aspen, Pam and the children moved to a very affluent area. But, she was struggling to pay the bills and maintain the lifestyle she was used to. Pam wanted to develop a new reputation away from Triano. So, even though she could not afford it, she continued to attend the fancy parties and socialised with the richest members of the Aspen community. Pam tried to get back into real estate, but this proved harder than anticipated because she didn't have the same well established connections as in Arizona. Pam started her own business, Star Babies, predicting the futures of new-borns. She firmly believed that this business could be worth millions, but she needed help.

This is when Pam met Ron Young. Young was supposedly working as a business consultant, although this doesn't appear to have been official. Young helped Pam with her finances, including with the Star Babies business. The two developed a romantic relationship and Young also became involved in Pam's ongoing communications with Triano about the divorce and money. Pam regularly complained about Triano not paying her enough in child support and maintenance. Young tried to help with this and saw Triano as an obstacle. Ron Young was very intelligent, but he was not particularly handsome or wealthy. Many friends wondered about Pam's motivations for the relationship; Young was not her usual type, so perhaps she had something else to gain from him.

By April 1996, Pam was going off Ron Young. Two separate reports had been made to police about Young, accusing him of fraud offences. Pam herself then contacted the police about him, claiming that he was using her credit card and stealing money from the Star Babies business.

Aspen detective, James Crowley, tried to locate Young, but he had disappeared. It transpired that a van was rented in Young's name from Aspen airport, but nobody knew where he had gone. An arrest warrant was issued due to the outstanding forgery charges.

Several months later, detective Crowley received a call from California – the van rented by Young had been located. Young mistakenly left the van near his parent's house and it had been impounded. When he attempted to recover the van, he was informed that the police had been contacted and were on their way. Upon hearing this, Young fled, abandoning the vehicle and its contents. Crowley flew to California to inspect the van and found several intriguing items inside. Such items included: papers from the Star Babies business, documents about Pam and Triano's divorce, a list of people close to Triano, maps of Tucson and hotel receipts in a fake name, also from Tucson. In addition, Crowley found a stolen Arizona licence plate and a sawn off shot gun. These things all seemed highly suspicious to Crowley and suggested that, for whatever reason, Young had been stalking Triano. Despite a wide police search, Young was still untraceable. There was little police could do.

Only two weeks after the discovery of Young's van, headline news stories appeared about a murder in Arizona.

On the 1st November 1996, Gary Triano had played a long round of golf with some friends at La Paloma Country Club. Triano was a member and regularly played 18 holes. Friends state that he was on the verge of being kicked out though, due to not being able to pay the membership fees. After the round of golf, Triano casually walked back to his Lincoln Town car. It was days away from his 53rd birthday and he was planning to celebrate in style. However, someone was waiting for Triano in the car park that day, finger poised. As he climbed into the vehicle, Triano noticed a blue bag that he didn't recognise on the passenger seat next to him. Curious, he reached over to investigate. At that moment, a bomb detonated, blowing the roof off the car and shooting the wind shield over 70 feet. Gary Triano was killed instantly, his wrist watch stopped at 5.38pm.

Emergency vehicles arrived quickly on the scene, but there was nothing they could do to help Triano. The local community of Tucson was in shock. No one could believe that a car bombing would take place there, especially at the most prestigious spot in town. Rumours started spreading that it must be an organised crime job; maybe the Mexican Mafia, or some other criminal that Triano owed money to.

Detective James Gamber collected evidence at the crime scene. Shrapnel and debris were everywhere, the first job was to separate pieces of the bomb from car parts. Eventually the bomb squad claimed that the device was a simple pipe bomb, detonated using a close range remote control from within a quarter of a mile. This meant that the killer was very nearby, probably within the car park, when the explosion was triggered. Although there were many rumours that it was a mob hit, the police had their doubts. The device was clearly built by an amateur, whereas organized crime groups usually employed experts for that type of job. Things didn't quite add up for detective Gamber.

When detective James Crowley in Aspen saw the news stories about Triano's murder, he instantly thought of the mysterious contents of Young's van. Wandering if the two incidents were connected, Crowley called police in Tucson to report his previous findings.

Pam, who was still living in Aspen, was questioned about her relationship with Young. She claimed that there had been no romantic feelings between the two of them, and that he had simply helped her out with financial advice for the Star Babies business. Pam also denied any knowledge of why Young would have suspicious items in his van and confirmed that she did not know his current whereabouts. Detectives could pin Young in Tucson in June and July 1996, thanks to documents found in the van, but they had no real evidence that he had been there in November when the murder was committed. Police did want to question Young in relation to the murder though, particularly because he had no other known connections with Tucson —so why would he get a hotel room there under a fake name? But, still, Young could not be found.

Pam herself was questioned further when detectives discovered that she was the beneficiary of a 2 million dollar life insurance pay out. However, Pam was very cooperative with police and there was nothing to suggest that she was a suspect. With no further leads, and police unable to locate Young, the case went cold.

Pam received the 2 million dollar life insurance money a couple of months after Triano's murder. She bought a large house in the wealthy neighbourhood of Meadowood, Aspen, and spent a significant amount remodelling it. Her lifestyle remained frivolous; partying, travelling, and skiing a lot. She was now able to fund her socialite habits comfortably again. Ten years passed in this manner, with no sign of Young, and Pam living a charmed life thanks to her ex-husbands murder.

In 2005, detective James Gamber, Pima County Sheriff, was assigned to work on unsolved murder cases. He had also worked on the original inquiry into Triano's murder, and felt compelled to look at the case again. There were over 300,000 pages about the car bombing to search through. Having checked everything thoroughly, Gamber concluded that there was only one line of inquiry that hadn't been followed through, one suspect that Gamber couldn't eliminate, and that was Ron Young. By this time, Young had been a fugitive for 9 years. Gamber contacted the popular show *America's Most Wanted* and persuaded them to run a show about Young. The episode aired on the 19th November 2005.

Following the show, police received a number of calls about Young. Most notably, one call was from his chiropractor in Florida, who had recognised him immediately. The chiropractor informed police that Young actually had an upcoming appointment scheduled. Police moved quickly, and on the date of Young's appointment, they were sat in wait. Florida police were then able to arrest Young on outstanding fraud charges.

Young spent 10 months in jail in Florida for fraud, before police were able to question him about the murder of Gary Triano. Young gave police permission to search his house, storage, and car. This turned out to be quite a bizarre experience for police. It quickly became apparent that Young was obsessed with keeping records, noting down interactions, recording phone conversations, and saving emails. His house was a veritable treasure trove of evidence. Of course, it took police a while to comb through everything. But what they eventually found turned out to be very incriminating; it implicated not only Young, but also Pam Phillips in the murder of Triano.

A large number of cassette tapes held recordings of phone conversations between Young and Pam. There were over 500 calls recorded, spanning a time frame of 8 years. In addition to the voice recordings, there were also 100 saved emails between the two. In almost all their conversations, Pam and Young talked about their favourite topic – money. Police realised that Pam had been regularly sending money to Young. She would send cash via FedEx, and then call Young to inform him of the amount and the tracking number. Incredibly, Young recorded all of these calls – pretty much gathering the required evidence for police. Young even filled in spreadsheets, keeping track of the total amount of money that Pam had sent him. Overall, 44 transactions had been completed. Police found this highly suspicious, particularly because the amount of money discussed by Pam and Young always added up to 2 million, the same amount that Pam received in life insurance for Triano. It sounded like the pair had a pre-existing agreement. There were several points at which Pam and Young argued; during one episode Young even accused Pam of murder and threatened that she would end up in a women's prison. It seemed that Pam had fallen behind with the payments and Young was very angry about it. As far as police could see, there was only one explanation for what was said in the recordings and the transfer of so much money. On the 16th October 2008, Pam and Young were indicted for first degree murder.

Police ran into new problems when they tried to track down Pam. It turned out that she had gone to visit her daughter, who was at college in Switzerland. Upon hearing of Young's arrest and her own indictment, she failed to return. Switzerland would not extradite suspects who were facing cases in which they could be given the death penalty. So, for a time, Pam was safe in Switzerland. She even struck up a new relationship with a wealthy man. They stayed together on the shore of the stunning Lake Lugano. But Pam's fortunes were soon to change.

It was announced that the death penalty was being dropped, meaning that Switzerland could extradite Pam. However, the announcement was made publicly, and Pam was a step ahead of the Swiss police. She was now a fugitive, on the run in Europe.

Meanwhile, Young was put on trial in Tucson, Arizona. The prosecution leaned heavily on the cassette tapes found among Young's possessions. Young pleaded not guilty, saying that he left Aspen in 1996 on a driving holiday with his son. Then, when Young realised he was facing charges of fraud, he didn't think it was a big deal and did not return. Despite having been missing for 9 long years, Young claimed that he wasn't hiding at all, and had instead just been going about an ordinary life in Florida. When questioned about the 2 million dollars discussed in the calls with Pam, he simply explained that it was nothing to do with Triano's life insurance. Young stated that the amount just referred to some equity in real estate that he believed he was owed a portion of. The defence also pointed out that there was no concrete evidence placing Young in Tucson in November 1996. But, despite pleading not guilty, in March 2010, Young was found guilty of first degree murder. The strong circumstantial evidence proved to be enough for the jury to agree. Young appeared to be extremely shocked by this decision. Six weeks later, he was sentenced to two back to back life sentences.

During Young's trial, police felt significant pressure to find Pam. Finally, thanks to European police and the intervention of Interpol, they were able to do so. Pam was discovered in Lichtenstein, before being tracked as she travelled to Vienna, Austria. This is where she was apprehended, on an American arrest warrant.

In July 2010, Pam was returned to Tucson. Her appearance had changed drastically, she looked much older and a little dishevelled. Pam was deemed unfit to stand trial, due to mental health problems. She was held at Pima County Jail, with a 5 million dollar bail set, while she received psychiatric treatment. Eventually, in October 2012, Pam was given the all clear, and a date could be set for the trial.

Pam was charged with first degree murder and conspiracy to commit murder. Her trial began on the 18th February 2014. The trial lasted for a total of 7 weeks, during which the jury heard entirely opposing arguments from the prosecution and the defence.

Again, the prosecution relied almost entirely on the circumstantial evidence provided by Ron Young's records. Pam was painted as someone who lacks empathy and is motivated only by greed. The defence saw it very differently; claiming that the only thing the prosecution had proved was that Pam and Young had some kind of financial link. There were no other facts. Pam's attorney, Paul Eckerstrom, pointed out that Pam wasn't even the one paying for Triano's life insurance – that had fallen to a friend in Aspen during Pam's earlier financial troubles. In addition, the insurance payment directly before Triano's death was missed, forgotten. This is an unlikely mistake to make if you were planning a murder, surely the suspect would have done everything possible to ensure that the insurance would actually be paid.

The defence also refer to the findings from DNA tests done on the pipe bomb, saying that the tests excluded Young from being the builder and perpetrator. This would naturally call into question Pam's involvement too.

The defence took their argument even further by providing an alternative suspect, Neil McNeice. A wealthy man who was addicted to cocaine and heroin, McNeice had already passed away in 2002. He was never fully investigated, and the defence claimed that this was an error on the part of the police. The story went that Triano had needed some cash, so he struck a deal with Neil McNeice, selling him a $250,000 diamond engagement ring. The problem was that the ring was a fake and only really worth around $9000. When McNeice realised this, he apparently flew into a rage, raving about how he would have Triano killed. McNeice's doctor, Lawrence D'Antonio, corroborated this, explaining that he had heard McNeice threaten to kill Triano on several separate occasions. D'Antonio clearly believed that McNeice was behind the murder.

Finally, the defence argued that Young's tapes had never been authenticated and that if the jury listened to them carefully all the way through, a different picture would be formed. Eckerstrom said that when Young accused Pam of murder, he was not talking about Triano, but about himself. Young was suffering from an illness at the time and needed the money for healthcare. Also, according to Eckerstrom, the 2 million dollars discussed was from real estate investments, as Young claimed in his trial. Eckerstrom gave an impassioned defence of Pam, and advocated for Young's innocence too, but the prosecution were about to react strongly.

With regards to the McNeice argument, prosecutors pointed out that the initial betrayal with the ring had taken place in 1991. It was a long time to wait to commit murder, especially for a powerful man who could have ordered something like that to happen very quickly. Prosecutors said that the defence had only shown that McNeice was angry with Triano, they had given no evidence that he was actually involved in the murder.

Next, the prosecution called their most prominent witness, an old friend of Pam's, Laura Chapman. Chapman's account would prove to be a deciding factor in the outcome of the trial. Chapman claimed that when Pam was living in Aspen, Triano went to her house one night and threatened her. The ex-husband and wife ended up having a huge argument. After Triano left, Pam apparently called Chapman and another friend, who both went to see if she was OK. Whilst they tried to console Pam, she told them about the 2 million dollar life insurance policy and said that she should just hire a hitman and have Triano killed. When Chapman learned what happened on the 1st November 1996, her first thought was one of horror that Pam had followed through with her plan. Chapman had apparently spent the following years living in fear that if she spoke about Pam's threat, something would happen to her.

Defence lawyers tried to claim that Pam had only said those things because she was upset and scared after the fiery argument with Triano. Also, the other friend who attended Pam's house that night has no apparent recollection of Pam talking about the life insurance and threatening to kill Triano. The prosecution and Chapman argued that the other friend is simply too afraid to testify against Pam.

In the closing statements, prosecutor Rick Unklesbay stated that Young was "not getting paid for business advice that she never takes, he's getting paid for murder."

After a long trial, the jury only took 3 days to decide Pam's fate. On the 8th April 2014, she was found guilty of murder. Sentencing took place on the 22nd May 2014. Pam entered the courtroom in shackles and an orange jumpsuit, not quite the designer brands that she was accustomed to. The prosecution pushed for the maximum sentence. Pam was awarded natural life in prison, with no possibility of parole. Judge Richard Fields stressed that he had "no residual doubt" about Pam's guilt.

Upon hearing her sentence, Pam stood and addressed the court. She repeatedly claimed to be innocent and described the whole experience as a nightmare. Defence lawyer, Eckerstrom, also remains convinced of Pam's innocence, "this is one of the hardest things I have ever had to do in my career, watch my client be sentenced when I know she is innocent." Eckerstrom described Pam's conviction as an injustice.

On the contrary, Heather Triano, Gary Triano's daughter from his first marriage, believes that justice has been served. She said that "Pam, who at one time was my stepmother and my friend, destroyed lives due to her greed and love of money." Trevor and Lois Triano, Pam's children, were not in the courtroom. When asked about them, Heather stated that "Pam's lack of thought for her own children is appalling." Heather Triano and other family members maintain that Gary Triano was a family man who loved his children. This is very different from Pam's account of an abusive, paranoid man, heavily involved in the Arizona mob scene.

Eckerstrom continues to fight and appeal Pam's case. But, nearly 18 years after the murder of Gary Triano, Pam Phillips was incarcerated and it is unlikely that she will ever be released.

HUSBAND KILLER : THE TRUE STORY OF LARISSA SCHUSTER

80

ERIN EDWARDS

Larissa Leann Foreman was born January 1, 1960. She grew up on a farm near Clarence Missouri. By all accounts she had a happy childhood. She won first place at the Randolph pony show, her father, Charles, won first place in the men's division and Deeann, her mom, won second in the bareback for pleasure division. Her parents seemed to be very involved in her life. She excelled academically; she was athletic and went after what she wanted with everything she had. She was described as a 'go getter'.

Larissa graduated High school and went on to the University of Missouri Columbia to become a biochemist. She didn't come from a rich family so she would work as a nursing aide at Boone Hospital Center in Columbia Missouri. It's not known whether she liked her work as an aide, however she did like a nurse named Tim Schuster, and he liked her as well. She was electrifying and intoxicating, Tim was enthralled. They started dating after becoming friends and just hanging out together after work.

Finally, in 1982 Tim popped the question, and Larissa said yes. Between 1982 and the birth of their second child Tyler in 1990 there was a whirlwind of things happening. There was the wedding in '82, the birth of their first child, Kristin, and a move to sunny central California, Fresno to be exact.

In the beginning Tim managed the cardiology Department for St Agnes Medical Center. While Larissa worked for Pan Agricultural Laboratories. Larissa saw the company declining and thought it a good time to start her own company; Central California Research Lab. She was ambitious and worked long hours to make her company a success. Tim continued to work at St Agnes and be both Mom and Dad to their two children.

According to friends Bob and Mary Solis, Tim was the one who made sure doctor appointments were kept, homework was done and dinner was cooked and on the table. Larissa ruled her house and Tim having a non-confrontational personality went along with her, if for no other reason than to keep the peace. By this time she was making more than twice what Tim made. It was her money that made it possible for them to move to Clovis and buy a much larger home than the one they had in Fresno. It looked like they had it all...but did they?

By this time Kristen was a teenager and as with most teens there was attitude. Kristen fought with her mother at almost every turn. She stood up to Larissa in such a way that she felt she had no other option than to send her daughter to her parents in Clarence, Missouri. Tim was upset that his wife didn't even discuss this move with him; she'd decided this IS what will happen. And soon his beloved little girl was gone. But still Tim kept quiet.

The Schuster's entered into a bitter, rancorous separation in 2002, after nearly 20 years of marriage and two children. They tried living in the same house after the separation. However Larissa was not happy with this arrangement. From the very beginning she didn't want Tim to have anything to do with Tyler, no visitation and no kind of a relationship with his son at all. This was not okay with Tim. On more than one occasion she made the statement that she wished Tim would just die.

In late June or early July Larissa took Tyler and went on a trip out of state. Tim took this opportunity to secure a condo and move out of the family's home. Larissa was livid that he would have the nerve to leave while she was away and accused him of taking things from the house that didn't belong to him. What earlier seemed like idle threats became something more, she told a neighbor that she should just get it over with and kill Tim herself.

A Plan started formulating shortly after Tim moved out of the Clovis family home. Larissa asked James Fagone a lab assistant and Larissa's sometimes babysitter, sometimes whipping boy if he would help break in to Tim's house and help her get back somethings he took when he moved out. She felt he wasn't entitled to them and left messages on his answering machine telling him he'd better bring them back...or else.

After returning from a trip Tim came home to a house that had been burglarized and ransacked. One of the things missing...the very set of mixing bowls Larissa had had such a fit over. Who was her accomplice in the break-in...none other than James Fagone? Larissa wasn't shy about what they had done, she told her manicurist Terri Lopez, that after the break-in she would go back to Tim's house and sit in a chair and look around at what they had done. She also told Tami Belshay that "it gave her a feeling that was better than sex."

After the burglary the Schuster's relationship went even further downhill. Tim knew who had broken into his condo. Larissa's bitterness not only let her destroy things in the condo, but she even bragged about keying his truck. She said it made her happy every time she saw the marks on his truck. Tim seemed worried about what his estranged wife was capable of. He moved again, this time to a house in Clovis that had motion sensors and an alarm. He obtained a handgun and a permit to carry a concealed weapon. Larissa had told her manicurist Ms. Lopez that she prayed every night that Tim would just die. At one point Larissa told her that she could kill Tim and get away with it. She also asked one of the employees at CCRL if her boyfriend knew anyone that would kill Tim or at least rough him up. She'd made remarks like this before and all who heard them thought she was just venting because the divorce wasn't going the way she wanted it to. She said she would do anything to keep Tim from getting the business.

According to Bob and Mary Solis, Larissa would belittle and embarrass Tim in front friends and family alike. She seemed to relish the power she had over him.

In late June St Agnes let everyone know that there would be a round of layoffs coming and to be expecting it. Tim and his friend Mary Solis was on the short list to be let go. Larissa laughed when she heard the news. On July 9th Tim, Mary, her husband Bob and another friend Victor Uribe all had dinner together. The group broke up about 10pm that night, before Tim left the Solis' they had made arrangements to meet for breakfast the next morning. Tim never showed for his exit meeting or for breakfast. This worried Bob and Mary, it seems Tim was never late for anything, and if he thought he was going to be late he called. He was also supposed to pick up Tyler that evening.

His friends tried to reach Tim, calling his cell phone. Finally they called Uribe and told him that they couldn't reach Tim and would he go by the house and check on their friend. Uribe arrived at Tim's house and went inside. There didn't seem to be anything out of place, until he went to the bedroom. Tim's watch, wallet and cell phone were lying on the dresser. Uribe was now worried as well. Victor said "He never went anywhere without his cell, he kept it with him at all times, in case the kids needed him."

No one knew what had happened to Tim. The police refused to even take a missing person's report until he'd been missing 24 hours. July 10th when Tim had not been heard from in the allotted time Bob Solis filed the missing person's report. Officer John Willow from the Clovis Police Department responded to the call.

Willow found Tim's handgun under a cushion of a chair. He found Tim's cell phone in the bedroom and called all the numbers in his contacts to see if any of them had seen or heard from Mr. Schuster. When he called Larissa she said she hadn't heard from him either. He also talked to Terri Lopez and she relayed to Willow that the Schuster's were going through a rather nasty divorce. John Willow decided to turn the case over to Detectives Larry Kirkhart and Vincent Weibert.

When they entered Tim's home they noted some damage on the wall behind the chair where the gun was found earlier. They found a briefcase in the same room as the chair. Inside they found a microcassette recorder and tape. In the bedroom they found an answering machine that showed only one number, a cell phone number belonging to Larissa Schuster. Detective Kirkhart then asked Larissa to come to the police station for a chat about her missing husband.

During her interview with the detectives she told them that she and Tim were getting a divorce and that they did not communicate very well with each other. They asked her about her cell number being on the caller ID. She fabricated a story about being asleep on her couch and waking up to find she had pushed some buttons and maybe she had speed dialed Tim. They asked her if she had her phone with her and she said no. Kirkhart called for a pause in the interview and went to the parking lot to find Larissa's car. He looked in the window and saw a phone on the center console, dialed her number and the phone in the car rang.

Kirkhart went back to the interview room and asked Larissa to come with them to unlock her car and retrieve her phone. Back inside the station the interview resumed. The detective went through her contacts that she had on speed dial, none of them were Tim's number.

Larissa's whole demeanor changed, she was shaking and in the opinion of the detectives showing signs of deceit. She came clean and admitted that she had lied to the detectives and she knew she shouldn't have. She claimed she wasn't trying to be deceitful. None the less they let Schuster go home, for now. At this point in their investigation they still had no idea what had happened to Tim. Kirkhart had asked Larissa if she thought that Tim could just cash out some money and leave town, go camping or to Vegas to just get away. She told them she didn't think he would do that, that he wouldn't leave his son like that. This was still just a missing person case and most of Tim's friends thought that perhaps he had just had enough, the divorce, the custody battle, losing his job was to much for him to handle. Tami Belshay, Bob and Mary Solis and Victor Uribe were among those friends. The detectives were thinking the same thing at this point.

With no solid leads on Tim's whereabouts detectives Weibert and Kirkhart kept searching for some clue, however small that might give them some direction on finding Tim. Kirkhart was going through Tim's ledger provided to them by Larissa. And they came across a name they were familiar with...James Fagone. They knew his name because he was the one suspected of breaking into Tim's house with Larissa shortly after Tim moved out of the family home a year earlier. They also knew that he was an associate of sorts of Larissa's.

The following Monday Detectives Kirkhart and Daly called Fagone to come and talk with them. Vince Weibert thought that perhaps Fagone might have some "inside" information on Tim's disappearance.

It seems that Fagone was a babysitter for the Schuster's son Tyler, before and after their separation. James was a good kid according to his attorney Peter Jones. "He's an above average student, higher than a 4.0 grade point average...a gentle spirit."

Fagone was nervous during the police interview. He admitted that Larissa had him help her break into Tim's house and take back things that she didn't want him to have.

James told the detectives that Larissa was going around the house looking for things and he just wanted to get the TV and some other stuff so he wasn't paying attention to what she was doing. Obviously James was scared out of his mind by now, but they pressed him more telling him they "knew he was involved somehow" with Tim's disappearance. Fagone's determination not to tell what had happened, what him and Larissa Schuster had done crumbled.

Fagone confessed that he had been there the night that Tim went missing, that he had gone to his house with a weapon. James relayed to them that Larissa had paid him the $2000 to purchase a stun gun and that he could just keep the rest for himself.

So as the day wore on James conveyed the sordid details of the night in questions.

On the night that Tim lost his job at St Agnes and had dinner with a group of friends, James had done what he was told to do by Larissa, buy a stun gun. Later he would get the call from her (Larissa). She picked him up and went to Tim's house. James laid in wait in the darkness just outside of his door. He could hear Larissa on the phone telling Tim that Tyler wasn't feeling well and she needed him to come to the front door.

A few moments later Tim opened the front door and James sprung from the shadows and attacked him wrestling him to the ground. Tim was struggling; James was using the stun gun on him, on the arm at first, not sure where else he might have zapped him. Soon Tim stopped struggling and when James looked up he saw Larissa with a rag that had been soaked in chloroform.

Were the detectives hearing this right? Was Fagone confessing to the murder of Timothy Schuster? But if they were going to believe any of it they needed some kind of evidence. They asked about the stun gun again, and what had Fagone done with it. He told them he threw it in a portable toilet on the edge of town. The investigators found the stun gun, right where James told them it should be.

Now at the same time Fagone was being interviewed Clovis Police Department got a call from a woman saying that her boss ask her to do something that in retrospect seemed a little off, suspicious even. Her Boss...Larissa Schuster. Leslie Dodd had been instructed to rent a moving truck by her boss. She was told to use her personal credit card and rent it in her own name not her boss's. A year earlier Larissa had asked the same employee to rent a storage unit near Schuster's lab, again to do it in the employees name and with her personal credit card.

Jim Koch got the call to check it out. He went to the storage unit and walked down the hall. He had been told to look for a blue barrel. When he found Schuster's unit and opened the door "there was a very very strong odor." Koch said. "I had on a breathing apparatus and gloves."

He saw the blue barrel, he opened it.

Koch said in an interview, "And when I opened the barrel I—I saw something that was very, very shocking to me and I recognized immediately as human remains. There was a barrel that's over 3/4 of the way full of fluid and portions of—of—body protruding from the fluid. And the body was obviously decaying. It was placed in acid. And the acid was basically eating away at the body."

Had Larissa Schuster killed her husband and put him in the barrel? According to James Fagone, yes she had, and he had helped her and then watched as she poured a caustic solution in on top of Tim. Worst of all, Tim was probably still alive when the acid was poured on him and he was sealed inside the barrel.

Tim had been found, the truth had come out and the Clovis detectives were on their way to Missouri to arrest Larissa for the murder of her husband Tim. They met her at the airport where she had gone to see her family. According to the detectives that arrested her for the murder she didn't even ask what had happened to Tim or how he died.

Both James Fagone and Larissa Schuster were arrested and charged with 1st degree murder.

Now that the perpetrators of Tim Schuster's murder had been arrested it was time to take them to trial. The murder was committed in the early morning hours of July 10, 2003. There was a lot left to do before the trial could begin.

The Clovis police department had to finish gathering evidence, talk to friends and family to make sure that everything was done correctly. They wanted to make sure that Larissa and James would not be let go on a technicality.

The judge had to decide if he would make this a death penalty case or a life in prison without parole case. That would be decided later. The prosecutor had to prepare a rock solid case and present the evidence to a jury in a manner that would guarantee a conviction. The defense would also be talking to people on behalf of their clients. Find people that had nothing but good things to say about them in hopes of offsetting the horrible truths that would come out at trial.

The judge separated the cases and James and Larissa would be tried separately. James was tried first. His attorney portrayed James as a misguided man who hero worshipped Larissa.

He was found guilty and is now serving a life without parole sentence.

There was so much media coverage on Larissa that the defense asked and received a change of venue. Her trial was moved to Los Angeles.

Monday October 22, 2007 Larissa's trial started. Prosecutor Dennis Peterson relayed to the jury of 9 women and 3 men just how the murder went down. He told them that Tim was still alive when the acid was poured over him while he laid head first inside the blue barrel. Her motive? She didn't want to share anything that they built during their 19 ½ years of marriage. She felt Tim didn't deserve any part of the business, or home and didn't want him to have contact with their tween son, Tyler.

CCRL employees would also testify to the facts of the blue barrel being at the lab and the day Tim was reported missing went to look for it and it was gone. They also said that Larissa had said that she should just shove Tim in the barrel and get rid of him.

A large amount of Hydrochloric acid, 12 gallons and Sulfuric acid, 4 gallons was ordered for Schuster's lab, more than ever before. Leslie Dodd (nee Fichera) testified that, "that was more acid than the lab would use in a year."

Joseph Boatwright thought Larissa was joking when she asked "if he thought a body would fit in the blue barrel."

Juror's watched several hours of Larissa's police interview. She made Tim out to be controlling and having a volatile temper. After seeing that part of the interview Bob Solis testified to the contrary, that Tim was very calm and a non-violent, non-confrontational person.

In another part of the interview with Clovis Detectives Schuster stated that "she prayed that Tim would get over this hostility about the divorce." Her manicurist Terri Lopez told a different story. Lopez said that "she told me she prayed every night he would die."

A hair stylist Becky Holland sometimes did Larissa's hair. During those appointments Larissa would rant about Tim. Holland didn't think much about it because she knew they were going through a divorce. Later though she said the hateful remarks escalated, Holland told the court, "this is getting a little creepy. It was so intense."

The jurors got to hear just how intense it was when they got to hear message after message of Larissa calling her husband awful names and making threats about their children. The prosecutor used these recordings to make a point to the jury; Larissa was in a "murderous rage". Nuttall interjected that these messages were left on Tim's machine 7 months before the murder.

And with this the prosecution rested, hoping that they had proved their case. There was one witness that they really needed to be able to lockdown the case against Schuster, they needed James Fagone. The judge had barred his confession so the jury would never hear in his own words what happened July 10, 2003. But he refused to cooperate with Peterson because he had already filed his appeal. The only thing that might have helped Peterson is the fact that James Fagone had already been convicted of Tim's murder.

Nuttall began the defense's case by telling the jury that neither he nor his client could tell them what had happened to Tim because "we don't know". And since the jury heard nearly nothing about Fagone, Roger Nuttall blamed the murder on him. After all Fagone had already been found guilty of the murder Larissa was now on trial for. Nuttall said in his opening statements that "Tim was an angry man who belittled Larissa in over-compensation for his own failings as a husband and father." And that "he began stalking Larissa after the divorce proceedings started."

Now Defense attorney Nuttall brought in a stream of witnesses that would steer the blame away from his client.

He had a medical expert that said the victim's body was cut in half and that the police had completely missed a second crime scene and the evidence from there would have proved that Fagone and others were responsible for Tim's murder not Larissa.

Nuttall even had psychiatrist Stephen Estner on the stand. Estner said that, "My impression was that Mrs. Schuster was a very direct and assertive person, and Mr. Schuster was a more passive and nurturing personality. And I think they started butting heads over that."

Larissa Schuster took the stand in her own defense and adamantly denied the charges saying, "No, I did not kill my husband." Again James Fagone would have the whole murder put squarely on him. Schuster told the jury, ""I heard him say something like 'there had been an accident and Tim is dead.' I thought he was joking."

She said that the $2000 payment to Fagone was for babysitting Tyler and housesitting while she was away on vacation with her son. Schuster said the large amount of acid was for cleaning a large scale of lab glass. Schuster seemed to explain everything away poking holes in the prosecutor's case. Would it be enough to get an acquittal? Had she actually swayed the jury?

It seemed that the trial was plagued with problems, including accusations of juror misconduct. At least one juror was replaced by an alternate due to disruptive behavior. Another admonished for giving Larissa a 'thumbs up' after her testimony. And yet with all of that...it was time for the jury to deliberate of the weeks of testimony they'd heard.

It took a little more than two days for the jury to decide on a verdict.

Guilty of Murder with a special circumstance of financial gain. The verdict came exactly one year after Fagone's.

Roger Nuttall slowed the sentencing of Larissa Schuster while he tried to find reasons to ask for a new trial. He even used the argument that there may have been juror misconduct. Nuttall wanted to talk to the jurors but Ellison said no. Nuttall appealed and the District court of Appeals told Ellison to contact the jurors on Schuster's behalf. All the jurors and alternates refused to speak to her attorney.

So on May 8, 2008, five months after being found guilty of her estranged husband's murder Larissa Leeann Schuster was sentenced to life in prison without the possibility of parole. Judge Ellison also denied her request for a new trial.

At the sentencing a total of seven people stood up to make statements about how they had been affected by the murder of Timothy Allen Schuster.

Kristen, Tim and Larissa's oldest child and only daughter made an emotionally charged statement to and about her mother.

She called her mother a demon for "taking my father away." And told her. "I pray you're continually haunted at night by the sight and sound of my father fighting for his last breathing moments on this earth. I hope you toss and turn and have horrible nightmares visualizing the horrific act of violence you have committed. Maybe later in life I can learn to forgive you, but I doubt it. This is goodbye, not just for now, but forever. This is goodbye as your daughter."

Kristen was so devastated over her father's murder she reached out to a support group murdervictims.com. Several people shared their own experiences of losing a parent at a young age hoping she could find at least a little peace.

HUSBAND KILLER SHEENA EASTBURN

94

JAIMI WEST

Sheena Eastburn seemed to have the cards stacked against her from the start. She and Tim Eastburn were married young, when she had only just turned fifteen. The couple wed in 1990, although Tim was older, at twenty-one years of age. Talking many years later to the Joplin Globe, Alica Blevins- Sheena's mother- talked about how she should have guided her daughter's life differently, and put her on a different path.

"She was only 15 then. She was just a kid... Sheena was wild. I will admit that," she said. "For her and Tim, life was one big party. "She got herself in situations that got her into a lot of trouble. There were a lot of things that happened to her as a child that she never told me.

I just wish I could have done more for her when I had the chance. Maybe things would have turned out differently."

They were divorced a short two years later, which is often the case for couples married at such a young age.

While the divorce was described by friends as amicable, the couple maintained a sexual relationship over the years. Both were heavy drinkers, and took drugs together. In fact, whenever Sheena needed a fix, friends said, she would visit her ex-husband and provide sexual favours in return for drugs. The couple were still so close that they discussed remarriage.

Speaking about their relationship, Sheena would later say: "There were days when he loved me more than you could ever imagine and there were other days when we just fought. I was 15 years old when we got married. He was like a father and a husband to me. He was a wonderful man."

On or around November 1st, 1991, Sheena met Terry Banks for the first time, and the two immediately became close. When Banks learned of Sheena's continuing relationship with her ex-husband, however, he became "extremely possessive, jealous, and violent" according to court records. This was the catalyst for Tim's murder.

Tim Eastburn's murder

Tim was murdered using his own rifle, on November 19th 1992. He was shot in his own home in McDonald County, Missouri. The house is set a little back from the road, among the wooded hills common in McDonald County.

At the time of the murder, Sheena had only just turned seventeen, and her co-defendants were nineteen (Banks) and eighteen as well (Myers).

Two days previously, Sheena's co-defendants, Terry Banks and Matt Myers, had stolen Tim's gun- an AK-47- in a break-in along with a third man named Denashay, or 'D.J'. Johnson. They also took the chance to steal some of Tim's valuables, since stealing the gun on its own would have appeared suspicious.

The burglary took place only two weeks after Sheena had begun secretly dating her fellow co-defendant, Terry Banks. Tim and Sheena, Banks, Myers and Johnson were in fact all part of the same large circle of friends. In the time building up to the murder, the group had been drinking to excess and using drugs, a fact which probably gave the defendants the courage to do what they were about to do.

On the evening of November 19th, Sheena, Banks and Myers paid a visit to Tim at his home. It was only on that day that Sheena learned of the burglary at all; Myers and Banks had said they wanted to sell the gun- which would have fetched a good price- but Sheena convinced them not to, since it could be traced back to Tim through the serial number.

Sheena went in at first, alone, to talk with him. She asked him if he would like to come outside to take a ride on her motorbike, but he refused, saying that it was too late at night for him to want to go out.

At the time, Banks and Myers were hiding on the front porch. As Tim and Sheena continued talking, they walked through the house to the kitchen, where the pair kissed. It was only seconds later that Tim was shot with his own gun, through the window, by one of the pair outside. He quickly fell to the floor, and as he lay, Myers ran into the house to shoot him again to 'finish him off'. As he shot Tim for the second and final time, Sheena and Terry Banks ran from the house.

According to later interviews with Sheena, Tim's last words were "God forgive me for all my sins."

All three were arrested only days later, and each confessed separately to their role in Tim's murder. Each of their confessions were coherent, and none of the defendants contradicted the others with regards to their description of the day's events. However, Banks and Myers both claimed that Sheena had come up with the plot to murder Tim, a claim that she denied.

The Trial

Sheena was in prison for three years by the time she was finally put up for trial.

The facts of Tim Eastburn's murder were not challenged in court by either Terry Banks or Matt Myers. The only challenge made by Sheena was whether her actions were made after 'deliberation and cool reflection' or not- which is the metric by which murder in the first degree is judged under Missouri law. However, the defence also argued that Sheena did not necessarily understand her co-defendants' murderous intentions beforehand, a fact which also would have lessened the charge against her.

In testimony for her defence, Sheena claimed that she only learned of the burglary on the day of the murder itself. She believed that on the day that Tim died, the group of three were going to steal money and drugs from her ex-husband. She denied any knowledge of a plot to kill him. "I was supposed to go down there and get him out of the house, then we were going rob him for drugs and money."

They also planned to leave the gun at Tim's house after the robbery, rather than arouse suspicion by selling it. Sheena was quoted in interviews long after the trial, still standing by what she said. "The intent was to take back the gun that was stolen. They could track it down.

The timeline of the day's events suggested otherwise, however. Sheena's request for her ex-husband to follow her outside, and her bringing him to the kitchen with a window to the front of the house, suggested that she was trying to lead him to her death. At the very least, it was clear that it wasn't Sheena who fired the fatal shots from Tim's own gun. She claimed that Banks had shot him first in a fit of passion, after seeing the pair kiss. Myers had then delivered the final bullet.

After the shot was fired, Sheena said, "[w]e both dropped and when we dropped I crawled around to where he was, and I tried to stop the bleeding. There was nothing I could do." She was trying to paint a picture of innocence. She later talked about how she had tried to stop the bleeding with a towel and a sock that were lying nearby.

Over the course of the trial, extensive physical evidence was used in attempt to prove the group's guilt, almost sixty items in total. These included the rifle and the fragments of bullets found in Tim's body- which matched- and photo after photo of the crime scene.

D.J. Johnson also testified to the effect that the murder had been pre-meditated. He was actually a witness for the prosecution throughout the trial, as part of a plea bargain to help secure the verdicts of murder against the other three. As a result of his actions, he was given probation in connection to the charges of burglary against him, as he was part of the group that stole Tim's AK-47.

He testified that on the day of the murder itself, he overheard a three-way conversation between Myers, Banks and Sheena. In that conversation, Sheena discussed Tim with the others, claiming that he had raped her, and that she would love to see him dead. Banks, her then boyfriend, and Myers then both volunteered their services, according to Johnson. Sheena's attorneys made no attempt to discredit him, or disagree with any of his testimony.

The defence, however, argued that his testimony was unreliable due to its acquisition through a plea bargain. Johnson was offered freedom in exchange for his witness statements, and this perhaps did cast doubt on the truth of what he said. However, it was left for the jury to decide just what to make of his claims, and his statements formed a key part of the prosecution's case.

Prison Time

Whether the jury's decision would have been changed by any of this information must forever remain unknown. What they did decide, after a gruelling six hours, was that Sheena was guilty of first-degree murder.

Matt Myers was sentenced as the man who, according to the three confessions, had fired both of the fatal shots. Although he was only charged with second degree murder, among other offences related to Tim's murder (i.e. the burglary), he was sent to prison for a total of 67 years. Because of the murder being judged as of the second degree, he was eligible for parole throughout his sentence.

Terry Banks on the other hand, was sent to prison for life, on a charge of first degree murder. Sheena, too, was jailed with the same charge. The fact that Banks and Sheena were charged with first degree murder, whereas Myers (who fired one of the shots that killed Tim) wasn't, seems strange in hindsight. But Myers had made a plea bargain that saw him receive 'only' 67 years, but with the chance for parole in the future.

Indeed, Sheena's attorney filed a motion for post conviction relief in the immediate aftermath of the sentence, but this motion was denied.

"I really believed I was going to get second degree murder and I was accountable for that. I was okay with that," Sheena said in an interview, years later. She was visibly stunned when she learned of her sentence. "All I could hear was my mother in the courtroom... She was wailing," Sheena told KOAM TV. As part of the same news segment, Sheena's mother Alica Bleavins remembered the same scene: "I couldn't control it. When that's your child, and your only child, and your hands are tied..."

Terry Banks' story became more interesting in the year 2000, when he escaped from his maximum-security prison with the help of a guard. Lynnette Barnett smuggled Banks out in broad daylight, with the help of an old uniform and a fake ID. They were on the run for six weeks before they were caught. She was jailed for five years, with the help of video evidence and correspondence between her and Banks. She was, however, paroled within a year of her sentence.

Banks had another 16 years added to his sentence, although since he was already in prison for life with no option of parole, it makes little difference.

At the time of the escape, Sheena's mother said: "They put her on lock-down. They put her in the hole. They were going to leave her there until he was captured. The FBI, well, they were all over Sheena. She was the one who told them his dad was in Texas."

Signs of hope for Sheena?

There were several facts and allegations which weren't raised at trial, that in hindsight, should have been. Sheena's attorneys spoke publicly about how the outcome may have been completely different had they brought them up.

For one, IQ tests performed by Sheena in the buildup to the trial suggested that she would be incapable of organising the events as described by the prosecution.

There were also allegations that she had been raped by a McDonald County Jail when awaiting trial, and even taken to an abortion clinic. A guard who had been working there, Terrie Zornes, had been accused by Sheena of manipulating and raping her several times over the course of her time there. He had been 31, whereas she was still a minor.

Sheena claimed that he had taken her twice to the property room in 1994, and attacked her there. He was the only guard on duty at the time. According to interviews, Sheena had told her mother: "I told my mother that the officer had taken me to a property closet and had sex with me. She flipped out at that point. They locked me down in my cell.

Cut off my phone. I wasn't allowed to talk to anybody. They cut off my visitors."

Multiple reviews of the surveillance tape from the nights that Sheena alleged she had been raped gave suspicious results. While nothing of note happened, at one point in the recordings the clock would jump forward. "The hands on the clock jumped forward. A clock doesn't do that," The Sheriff of McDonald County Jail later said.

The Sherriff had nonetheless defended Zornes, claiming that the sex was "consensual". Altogether, it seemed as if both the guard and the Sheriff felt that there was something to hide.

Sheena responded with revealing comments about her past. "They kept trying to tell me it was consensual. They said: 'You know you wanted it. You know you miss it.' It was not like I fought it because there was no way I could have stopped him. I have experienced sexual abuse all of my life. I have been raped before in a violent way. After you have been in that situation, you just learn it's easier to let it go and not fight."

Moreover, in the years since the case was closed, Myers recanted on his testimony at the trial that Sheena had been the mastermind of the operation. Kent Gipson, Sheena's long time attorney, had even attained an affidavit to that effect- and that he had acquired the same from Johnson, too. This would mean that in conjunction with their defence stemming from the low IQ test score, it would be possible to argue that Sheena could not have possibly wanted Tim to be killed that day.

These facts all gave Sheena hope that she could appeal her sentence, and perhaps, win. Even if she were only able to replace her sentence with one for second degree murder, she would at least be eligible for parole in the end.

Supreme Court challenge

In interviews after her sentencing, Sheena said: "I still thought that I might get out of prison someday... I didn't realize that life without parole actually meant life without parole." She continued to maintain her innocence, saying that she had never planned a murder that day, only a robbery.

In 2012, a case went through the Alabama Supreme Court which found that the sentence of life without parole was actually unconstitutional when handed down to a minor. The case came from Alabama, but because it had been decided by the Supreme Court, cases could now be challenged nationwide. Missouri, at the time, had 84 cases of juveniles jailed for life without parole and each one of them could now seek to have their sentences reduced.

Suddenly, it seemed that Sheena might have found a way out. Once more, Sheena contacted her attorney, and they began to prepare her case for appeal. Talking to KOAM TV, her attorney Kent Gipson said "I think if you look across the spectrum of persons convicted of first degree murder, I'd say her level of culpability is among the lowest I've ever seen."

Sheena's attorney believed that she had a great chance to finally be considered for parole; and both clearly believed that she deserved the chance. "I think inevitably she will be given a parolable sentence and will be given a chance to get out of prison," Gipson said at the time. Speaking about the progress she had made while in prison, he said "She's obviously not the same person she was when she was 17 years old,I don't think any of us are... She is probably the most ideal candidate for parole any of them [prison staff] have ever seen.""

Miles Parks, a retired investigator who had worked on the case, disagreed. "Sheena Eastburn was old enough to get a driver's license, old enough to get married, old enough to know the difference between right and wrong," Parks said. "What do you think is the appropriate punishment?"

In an interview before her appeal with KOAM TV, she talked about the possibility that she might be released. "I came to that realization a long time ago, and I gave it to God, and I got peace," she had said. She still maintained that she had no role in Tim's murder, saying that "[t]here was no reason for Tim to die... None."

With her interviewer, she discussed what she missed about the outside world: "...going down to the refrigerator in the middle of the night and being able to get what you want. Walking barefoot on grass somewhere that it doesn't say 'out of bounds'. Going outside after dark. Just taking time to experience free, fresh air... I know it smells different on the other side."

Sheena wished that she could somehow find release. But she still refused to get her hopes up, stating that "You never count on anything completely until it happens because you can't let yourself get your hopes too high and then be devastated all the time. It's just a hard way to live." Over her time in prison, she had clearly lived with a hope that one day she would be set free, but had only been disappointed.

The Post-Conviction Hearing

Close friends and relatives of Tim's did not want the case re-opened. Speaking in an interview, Bobby Eastburn said, "We have been keeping track of it. We don't like what is going on. She worked hard to get in there and we don't want her out of prison. "My brother won't get a second chance. She's apparently trying to get a second chance. They say she was suffering from PTSD because of her childhood and that she was not very smart. She manipulated the situation to kill Tim. She was the mastermind behind it. She was intelligent enough to set the whole situation up."

On April 30th of 2013, three cases of minors jailed for life were put before the Missouri Supreme Court- one of them being Sheena's. Her attorney argued that the original motion that had been filed way back in 1992, for post conviction relief, should not have been denied. They argued that the judge should have then realised that such a sentence was unconstitutional.

The state argued that they did not then have the authority to challenge the constitutionality of the sentence, and so they were correct to not have allowed the defendant's motion for relief. After both sides had been presented, the court took recess so that the judges could decide on their fate.

"I am definitely guilty of second-degree murder," Sheena said in an interview around the time of her appeal.

But whether or not her appeals would be successful, she felt all along that she could never be free. "For somebody with a case like this, the prison is not really the prison. It's always going to be inside. You will always be in prison. It does not matter whether you are free or locked up, I think you will always have that inside."

But on Tuesday 25th July, that year, the Missouri Supreme Court returned the unanimous verdict that her appeal did not stand. Based on the facts of the case, they still argued that it was necessary for Sheena to be imprisoned for life.

Sheena's final hearing

It turned out that Sheena would eventually win her appeal after all.

In 2015, Sheena appealed again, under the same Supreme Court ruling as before. In her hearing of October that year, she sought the sentence of second degree murder through a plea agreement with the prosecutor. To do so, Eastburn had to waive any and all post-conviction and appeal rights- which she did.

The hearing was only 25 minutes long in total this time around. Lou Kelling, a former sheriff and supporter of Eastburn's release on parole, said at the appeal, "This is what she should have been charged with to begin with. She was an accessory to the crime. She served 10 years more time than she should have served. That on top of the fact that she was mistreated while in custody."

The defence had indeed used the same arguments as in the prior appeal, including the evidence of Sheena's IQ test, and allegations of rape and forced abortion. This time, the court decided to vacate the prior judgement. Since she had been in prison for more than 23 years, the agreement made her immediately eligible for a parole hearing.

Parole at last

Sheena Eastburn is now set to be released from prison in November, 2017. She has been judged to have served her time for second degree murder, and is getting ready for life on the outside for the first time in her life as an adult.

In a telephone interview with the Joplin Globe after it became common knowledge that she was set to be released, Eastburn said: "I now know when I will be able to move on with my life. I am grateful for a chance at parole."

In the same interview, she described how she was planning to write to the parole board and the governor in the hope that she could demonstrate just how much she had changed during her time locked away from society. "I want to show that I can be successful outside of the prison," she said. "I am very sorry for the things that happened. I have changed my life and will make better choices."

In another interview, she described her plans for the outside world. "I would go to school to become a certified personal trainer. I would love to minister to juveniles and help them know that the choices we do make have a consequence. I really do want to help people. I know that sounds crazy. But I want to help and let them know there are other choices out there no matter what your life is like because I had a bad life and childhood, but I still had choices. I did not realize that then."

And it did indeed seem that she had made genuine effort to turn her life around. In a separate interview, Sheena's mother claimed that her daughter had made every effort she possibly could from within the prison system. "Sheena has completed all of the classes that they offer at the prison. She has taken everything ... She'll sit there and the taxpayers will pay $80,000 a year to feed and house her. If she had been let out, she'd have a job and feed herself. This is something I don't understand. But we are still grateful to have a release date."

"We have waited a long time for this day to come, but we don't know when she will be released. We don't have an out day yet," Blevins said. "It could be just a matter of some paperwork. No one can really say right now."

During her time in prison, Sheena had begun full time work as an obedience trainer for rescue dogs. On top of this full time job, she had also become a qualified aerobics instructor, and found occasional work in prison helping disabled inmates. On occasion, she even led victim counselling sessions. She had spent her time as wisely as she could, and it had given her inspiration for her future release.

Before her first appeal on the unconstitutional nature of her sentence, her attorney had said "Maturity and education, things like that, should be taken into account and that's all we're really asking, that she be given the opportunity to prove to the parole board and other people that she deserves a second chance."

By the end of this year, she will be getting that chance.

HUSBAND KILLER SHARI TOBYNE

ANA BENSON

When it comes to female killers, the most common type of crime is mariticide or murdering their husbands. There are many motivations behind taking someone's life but killing a person so close to you is often fueled by passion, financial gain, jealousy, or betrayal. The case of Shari Tobyne is the perfect example of a woman scorned. Her husband of thirty-five years wanted to divorce her due to the financial problems she caused by mishandling the couple's finances.

So one day before he was set to leave their rented house and move on, Shari snapped. She simply couldn't allow him to leave after so many years they spend together. Shari continued to live her life normally, but Arizona police started uncovering body parts from counties surrounding the city of Phoenix and they couldn't determine the exact identity of the deceased man. Worried Tobyne children alerted the law enforcement that their father was missing and this is where the story started to unravel.

It will soon be discovered that a loving mother and a grandmother murdered her husband in cold blood because leaving him was simply not an option.

Early life

Shari Tobyne was born on 24th of July, 1956 in Clifton, Kansas. She grew up in a rural area just outside of the city. Her parents owned a farm and her father was quite successful in his line of business. She was a happy, carefree girl who enjoyed spending time in nature and would often help her family by jumping in and completing difficult farm related tasks.

This is where she met her future husband, Dwight Tobyne. He lived just across the street from Shari and his parents ran their own agricultural business. Dwight loved Shari's personality and energy so he soon realized that he had a crush on her. However, he didn't want to make a move too quickly so he waited until he got a college acceptance letter to ask Shari to be his girlfriend. She was still in high school at that time.

Both Shari and Dwight wanted to achieve business success and escape their small town. They soon realized that they were a match made in heaven because they cheered each other on and offered great support when needed. The couple married in 1975 and they made a decision to move to Salina, Kansas to start their life as a husband and wife. They wanted to make a better future for their family and relocating to a big city was their best option.

Shari was a bit apprehensive at first but the fact that she had Dwight right there beside her made the transition a lot easier. Dwight started a semester at the University of Kansas, studying Animal Sciences while Shari wanted to be a perfect wife and keep their home in pristine conditions. The pressure was on Dwight and he simply had to succeed with his academic work because he was supposed to carry the Tobyne family to the business success eventually.

The couple's first child, Jennifer was born in 1977. They welcomed a baby boy, Brad only three years later. The family was growing but Dwight was still in college, trying to graduate. Shari was very stressed about the financial situation and they struggled to take care of their children. Dwight did his best to earn some extra money so he landed a part-time job in hopes it would cover the expenses.

Trading stocks and interests were all the rage back in the 1980s and Dwight though it would be a perfect opportunity to invest the money he had on his account and try his luck. It wasn't his field of study and he soon got lost in all the numbers and investment opportunities. He pretty much gambled away all of their family savings and they ended up getting evicted from their townhouse. They packed their things and moved back to their parents.

With a third child on its way, the Tobyne family was under a lot of stress. Dwight even though about leaving Shari because he felt like he had failed both her and their children. Being the provider was already very hard for him and the fact that he managed to spend all of their money created additional pressure. Moving back to their parents was another blow. The situation was dismal and both of them knew that they have to make some difficult decisions in near future.

The move and success

The Tobyne family wanted to have a new beginning so they packed their things and moved to Denver, Colorado. Dwight was ecstatic because he can continue his education up there and earn a master's degree that will certainly come in handy when it comes to finding employment in near future. He also landed a full-time job at a bank and the pay was quite good.

Inspired by the economic boom of the 1990s, Dwight Tobyne enrolled into a business school and earned a diploma after a couple of years. Combining everything he learned with smart ideas and investments, Dwight created a leasing company. It was exactly what Denver needed at the time and he knew it would be a success.

It took Dwight a few years to make some serious money and now the family was living comfortably in a large house. They had everything imaginable and Shari finally started to feel confident. She knew that Dwight was a hard worker but she did have doubts when the company was first started because she knew how it felt to lose money.

The Tobynes looked like a perfect family because they were wealthy, active in the community, and their children were successful in school. Shari loved the attention and enjoyed a classy lifestyle that was a complete opposite of the things they went through in Kansas. She felt the need to contribute to the wealth of her family so she got her real estate license. It was time to stop being a housewife and start doing things on her own.

Dwight supported his wife's decision to create her own business and they cheered each other on as usual. They would often collaborate and help each other out with work-related tasks. Everything seemed to go really well for the Tobynes and they continued to live large with their ever-growing wealth.

The first sign of trouble

In 2003, Shari and Dwight lived alone in their family house. The children have moved out and the two of them still ran their business successfully. One day, Shari told Dwight that she made some mistakes regarding one of her accounts and that the numbers were not adding up. Her client lost their money due to this mistake and Shari's real estate license was taken away. Her job and the real estate career were in jeopardy.

It was clear that Shari tried to commit some type of fraud but she was never prosecuted for that. The Tobynes had plenty of money left in the bank and since they were experts at the new beginnings, they thought it would be the perfect time to move somewhere warmer. Dwight told his friends that they were going to Arizona because the real estate opportunities down there are amazing. But the truth was they were fleeing the city because the majority of their neighbors were aware of Shari's bad business decisions and they needed to surround themselves with people who don't know them well.

They bought a huge house in Gilbert, Arizona which was as posh and classy as their previous residence. It was a part of a gated community outside of Phoenix and they felt right at home. Dwight continued with his leasing business and it seemed like Phoenix was really a good relocation choice because he was getting a lot of work there. Since Shari was not employed, she became very involved with the way Dwight ran his business. She started helping him out because she had plenty of free time on her hands. Shari was in charge of family finances.

But in 2008, Dwight started getting phone calls from his friends and clients who were asking about his health. The majority of them though that he was in a hospital. Dwight figured out that Shari was behind this and that she was telling them that he had a heart-attack. He got really worried and started going through his company's financial records. He noticed something alarming – he was missing a large amount of money and since Shari was in charge of the accounts, he asked her about it.

The confrontation was quite explosive, mostly because Dwight couldn't believe that she could do something like that to him. After all, they have been married for decades and stealing from his own company was simply shocking. Shari had an explanation for everything and she told Dwight that she took the money to pay the bills and other necessities. Dwight was still unconvinced and furious. He knew what she had done in Denver and this looked almost the same.

Just a couple of weeks after the fight, Shari contacted her children and she sounded distracted. They weren't sure what was happening but it was clear that something was very wrong. Dwight was at the house when he realized that he hadn't seen his wife for hours. After combing every room of their home, he went out to his neighbor's house and he found Shari laying on a couch. There was an empty pill bottle right beside her. Shari wasn't responding and he called an ambulance.

Once she was conscious, Shari explained that she did try to kill herself because she simply couldn't take it any longer. She hid important information from Dwight and he found everything out in the hospital. They were in serious debt and their accounts were pretty much emptied out. The reality came crashing down on Dwight and he couldn't hide the sadness from his face. His business was ruined and he worked hard for nothing. He was still in disbelief that his own wife could have done this.

The Tobynes had to sell their lavish house in the gated community in order to cover at least a portion of the debt. It was a psychological shock to both of them because they had to find a smaller place to live in. They were back at the square one. So they gathered their things and moved to Scottsdale, Arizona.

The tensions between the pair were high and Dwight was on the fence about divorcing Shari. He made a decision to leave her in autumn of 2009 because he couldn't forget the things she put him through.

However, they did their best to appear as normal as possible in front of their children. But when Dwight failed to show up at the Thanksgiving dinner in November of 2009, Shari confessed that Dwight left her and moved to Mexico. None of their children could have predicted that Shari was not telling the truth about the divorce and that the reality was more sinister.

The murder of Dwight Tobyne

In November of 2009, Shari bought herself a gun. She started practicing shooting at a local gun range and her last visit to that place was on 22nd of November. It looked like the divorce was the final straw that made her think about murdering her own husband. After getting a sense of how the gun worked, all she needed to do is find the right time to shoot Dwight. The exact date of the murder is still unknown but sometime between 24th and 28th of November 2009, Shari entered the couple's bedroom and fired the gun at Dwight Tobyne. It is presumed that she shot him in the head.

She then wrapped his lifeless body into the carpet that was already soaking up the blood and dragged him to a garage where she proceeded to chop his corpse into pieces. She took her time with each and every part, first cutting off the arms and feet. She did use a saw, as well as some other tools, but Shari also tore away some pieces herself. The garage was a mess and she needed to get rid of every single evidence that could connect her to the murder.

After wrapping the parts into cellophane and carpet cutouts, she loaded them up in her car and started making rounds through adjacent counties, dropping them in remote areas by an interstate. She did her best to leave them a bit away from the road in hopes that the animals would drag the parts even further into the wilderness. She was certain that this was the way to keep the police off her trail and ensure that she will not get caught. She then cleaned the crime scene with plenty of bleach, removing each and every spec of blood from the floor and walls. She presumably got rid of the saw and other tools as well.

She kept Dwight's cell phone and intended to pretend like he simply left her. She planned to contact her children every now and then via text messages and e-mails so they would think that Dwight was alive and well, soaking up the sun in Mexico. Since Shari wouldn't make any profit from her husband's death, the only explanation was that this was a crime of passion. They were married for almost thirty-five years and Dwight simply couldn't leave her right then after everything they went through. Shari's emotions obviously get the best of her and the result was gruesome.

The discovery of the crime

Even though Dwight missed the Thanksgiving dinner, the biggest red flag was the fact that he wasn't present at the birth of the Tobyne's second grandchild. He did contact his children via text messages so they though he was alive and well. But when he didn't show up at the hospital, his oldest daughter alerted the police. It was July of 2010 and the law enforcement immediately started working on this case.

The Tobyne children told the authorities that their father wanted to move to Oklahoma but their mother told them that he went to Mexico. The investigators were certain that the story was false so they focused their attention on Shari since she was the last known person to see him alive. She was living with her children at the time because she had to move out from the condo she shared with her husband and didn't have enough money to support herself on her own. When they brought Shari for the first interview, she denied everything. Shari told them that she had no idea where her husband was at the moment and that he hadn't contacted her in months.

She was released but the police investigators did sense that something was very wrong with her statements. They decided to put her under surveillance in order to see what she would do next and monitor any possible suspicious activities. Just like it was expected, Shari started acting oddly. The police officers saw her disposing of something in a dumpster and when they got there, they discovered a couple of clothing items, as well as pieces of a gun. She then proceeded to clean the trunk of her car which was even more alarming to the detectives because it looked like she was getting rid of the possible evidence.

Then they managed to locate Dwight's Ford pickup truck at a parking lot. It was obvious that the car was there for months but no one had reported it because it was parked in front of a residential building and there were a lot of vehicles there on a daily basis. There was no physical evidence of the crime anywhere in the car which meant that Shari probably didn't use it for body disposal. Checking the cell phone records was the next step and the investigators discovered that both of their phones were at the same location during the time frame when the possible murder occurred, as well as afterward. So Shari's story about Dwight leaving for Mexico in November of 2009 was clearly false because he wouldn't leave his phone behind. It was time to bring her back to the station for a second interview.

Shari broke down under pressure and told the detectives a whole new story. She said that she bought the gun with an intention to use in for her own suicide. Shari was feeling horrible after everything she had done with her husband's money and she wanted to end her life. The fact that Dwight was leaving her added to her depression and she simply couldn't continue to live anymore.

She brought the gun to their bedroom wanting to shoot herself in the head. Instead, Dwight who was there as well noticed the gun, grabbed it from her hands and unintentionally pulled the trigger while they were fighting for the weapon. He shot himself and was losing a lot of blood quickly. He was soon dead. Shari then said that she was lost and scared, knowing that no one would believe her story. So she quickly wrapped her husband in the sheets and dragged him to her car. She drove off to a remote location and left his body there.

Shari insisted that the death was an accident and that she didn't mean to hurt her husband. She volunteered to take the investigators to the place where she dumped the body. Listening to her directions, they went east of Scottsdale and started combing through the area. They couldn't find any traces of Dwight's corpse even though they covered a wide field around the alleged dump site. They knew that a lot of time has passed since the killing and that animals could have dragged the body someplace else, but they couldn't find anything that could indicate that a corpse was there in the first place.

The investigators placed Shari in the jail and continued to question other possible witnesses that could shed some light on this case. It was obvious that Shari's story was either incomplete or entirely false. They approached the owner of the apartment which Tobyne's were renting at the time of the murder. She told the police that the carpet in the master bedroom was brand new after Shari left the condo and that she also noticed a strong smell of bleach in the garage. It was a minor clue at the time because the investigators knew that Shari was an obsessive cleaner and she would often go around the house with pure bleach in order to disinfect all the surfaces. However, once they put the pieces back together, the bleach will play an important part in the investigation because it was used to clean up the scene.

Finding Dwight Tobyne

Back in December of 2009, prior to the missing person report which was filed by Dwight's children, dismembered body parts were found near a highway in Pinal County, namely legs without feet. The cuts were partially clean but they could see that the murderer did apply some force and they were more focused on tearing off the limbs than on keeping everything pristine. The police officers were sure that a saw of some kind was used in the process. The parts were collected by the police and sent for further analysis. The second set of body parts was discovered in La Paz County only a couple of days later. Hikers bumped onto a man's torso near the main road and alerted the authorities who once again collected the evidence.

Two police departments got into contact and they examined their findings in order to determine that the parts belonged to the same person. And then, three days later, a person traveling on a motorbike noticed something strange on the side of the road near Sugarloaf exit. The authorities in the area were already aware that they had a dismembered body on their hands and the remains were transported to Pinal County to make sure they also came from the same victim. The results were positive but the identity of the man was still unknown because they hadn't found the hands so fingerprint search was out of the question. As a matter of fact, some remains are still missing to this day.

The investigators who were working on Dwight Tobyne's case were aware of the mystery man who was found in three counties and they took a DNA swab from his parents in order to see if it was the match. The dates of the discoveries overlapped their murder theory and the detectives feared the worst. But before they delivered it to the medical examiner's office, they compared Dwight's physical description with the collected body parts. Hugh Lockerby, a detective from Scottsdale who worked on this case said: "A left leg was recovered first. A couple of days later, north of Phoenix, right leg was discovered. One hundred miles west of Phoenix a complete torso was uncovered. I asked could they give me a little description of the race, the height, the weight, and I am listening as they are telling me this and that is the exact description of Dwight Tobyne."

When the tests came back positive, they confirmed that it was, in fact, Dwight Tobyne. Since Shari Tobyne didn't mention any dismemberment of the body in her second statement, they had enough evidence to prove that she was lying. It was time to confront her and try to find out what exactly happened on that fatal night in November of 2009.

Shari pleaded not guilty in front of a judge and repeated her story about the accidental shooting. Her lawyer, Anne Phillips asked the judge to allow a psychological evaluation of her client because she was impossible to communicate with. She refused to provide her with any helpful details and Phillips thought that Shari might need some psychological help due to the fact that she was suicidal in the past.

Her attorney also wanted to be sure that Shari Tobyne did understand the charges properly. It looked like she was not fully there and her responses were sparse, providing Phillips with short answers only. The judge allowed a psychiatric examination and it was confirmed that Shari was responsive and aware of her actions. She didn't suffer from psychosis or depression. There were no underlying psychological issues and she was capable of attending her own trial.

However, the way she acted after the murder told the psychiatrist who conducted the evaluation that Shari Tobyne was a textbook sociopath. Not every person has the ability to separate their emotions and continue acting normally after a crime like this. She was sticking to her story no matter how unlikely it sounded and it seemed like Shari did really believe in her version of the shooting.

The trial

As previously mentioned, Shari Tobyne pleaded not guilty in the initial hearing. The state had a solid case against her even though they had no witnesses to the murder itself. She did confess to accidental shooting so she clearly was involved to some degree. However, her actions after the gun went off told a different story about a very violent body dismemberment and disposal. The fact that Shari lied to the authorities about the location of the body dump added a whole new layer to the case. She obviously didn't want the body to be found and hoped that the animals would do the dirty work for her.

Shari was facing the charges of a first-degree murder, as well as a concealment of the body parts. Since she did have some sketchy history regarding the financial fraud, the authorities had enough evidence to add it to the charges as well. They were asking for the death penalty. Shari's attorney didn't have much to work with but she repeated her old story about the accidental shooting. The verdict could have gone in both ways at that point, depending on the jury. So instead of going on a trial, Shari decided to end it as quickly as possible.

Shari Tobyne pleaded guilty on May 19th, 2012, ending the trial. It was the only way she could avoid the death penalty. That was a clever decision because her claims were simply not strong enough to convince everyone that she didn't shoot her husband on purpose. So instead she received life in prison and an additional thirty-one years for the financial fraud.

The children were in shock from the beginning of this case and they had a difficult time accepting the fact that their loving mother could actually kill their father. Shari Tobyne remains behind the bars and it is unclear when and if she would get an opportunity for an appeal.

HUSBAND KILLER DONNA YAKLICH

121

JESSI DIXON

Old-fashioned police work

In December 1985, a narcotics detective was shot and killed in the driveway of his farm in Pueblo, Colorado, where he lived with his five children and his wife, Donna Yaklich. Initially, authorities suspected Dennis' death was linked to his work in law enforcement, but a tip led them to two teenage shooters – and eventually, back to Dennis' wife, Donna.

However, attorneys for Donna Yaklich argued that Dennis had been beating his wife. The murder, they claimed, was a battered woman's desperate attempt to escape a lifetime of abuse – or potentially becoming a murder victim herself, like Dennis' first wife, who is thought to have died of a diet drug overdose in 1977.

Yaklich was finally acquitted of first-degree murder after a mistrial and a second trial that has been described as "grueling," but was convicted on the charge of conspiracy for hiring gunmen to kill her husband. Her sentence was forty years in prison, but was released to a halfway house in 2005, after serving close to eighteen years.

The young men Yaklich had hired to carry out the murder were also arrested and sentenced. Charles Greenwell, who was only 16 when the crime was committed, received a sentence of twenty years while his brother Eddie, who had been 25, received thirty years.

However, while Yaklich's claims of abuse weren't enough to get her off on the premise of self-defence, they did encourage authorities to reopen their investigation into the death of Barbara Yaklich. According to a cold case team, the investigation was "incomplete."

"This case needed some good, old-fashioned police work," said team lead Steve Johnson, with the Colorado Bureau of Investigation. "In my opinion, I have seen better documented traffic accidents."

Discrepancies were found in the autopsy report, which originally claimed Barbara had fainted from taking diet pills. When her body-builder husband, Dennis, tried "energetically" to resuscitate her, she suffered bleeding in her abdomen. However, administering CPR is not an appropriate reaction to fainting – and as a police officer trained in CPR, Dennis would have known this.

Still, there was apparently no examination of the potential crime scene, and when Dennis was asked to take a polygraph to support his defense, he refused.

Denver-area pathologist Michael Doberson determined that the conclusions in the report were "very unusual" – the internal damage Barbara had suffered, he claimed, was more likely caused by a blow to the abdomen. Doberson included his findings in a letter to Johnson dated in 2005, stating that in his opinion, "the entire scenario is simply not credible." A second forensic pathologist concurred with Doberson's conclusions.

According to reports, Barbara's liver tore open and her abdomen was quickly filled with more than 2,000 millilitres of blood – nearly 40 per cent of her total blood volume, and more than twice as much as is typical in a victim of a fatal car accident.

Investigators are now considering her death as "suspicious," with the tear caused by a blunt force trauma consistent with "punches and knee drops to the upper abdomen," according to pathologist Stephen Cina. However, the autopsy report showed no other indications that would reveal a pattern of abuse – no recorded discoloration, bruising, or external signs of beatings.

While the investigation into Barbara's death is now complete, the case hasn't been closed. According to the coroner and the Pueblo County Sheriff, the public deserves answers to the questions that have been raised.

The family man

Donna Yaklich met Dennis and his children only a few months after Barbara's death. According to Yaklich, the plan was to move in with the family for the summer and help him get the kids back into their home, since they were temporarily staying with Dennis' mother.

"I had no expected to fall in love with the children, who so desperately needed someone," Yaklich said. "They were grieving for their mother, so I couldn't bear to leave them."

Barbara had died on Valentine's Day, and had "appeared fine" as her children left for school that morning. However, an hour later, Barbara was dead – and Dennis was the only person who had been with her as she died. According to some reports, there are members of the community who do continue to question Dennis' involvement in the death of his first wife, including at least one of his former co-workers.

"Dennis' fellow officers knew he was out of control, but they also knew when they needed him he would be the first to go through the door," Yaklich said. "No one who worked with him would go against him."

It was this feeling of hopelessness that eventually led Yaklich to hire gunmen to kill her husband, in an effort to finally end the ongoing abuse. She'd moved in with Dennis when she was only 22 and he was 30. The children were aged 3, 9, 11, and 12 – and she immediately fell into the role of step-mother, despite the abuse which began only a month after Yaklich moved in. She said she attempted to leave a few times, but always went back.

"I feared Dennis, but at the same time I felt at home with him because I had grown up in an abusive environment," Yaklich said. "I fell into the trap of thinking if I could make everything perfect for him, he wouldn't get mad at me or at the kids. Dennis' threats to kill me or kill someone I loved if I ever left again kept me there."

Dennis even threatened to use his access to federal law enforcement agents against Yaklich, telling her that she'd never be able to get away from him – these agents were capable of fiding anyone, anywhere. Eventually, she said, "I lost myself. I lost hope."

"I became very depressed and mad at myself because I had no trusted my instincts about leaving the relationship when the abuse started," Yaklich said. "Suicidal thoughts became an answer. Then came homicidal thoughts."

Looking back, Yaklich admitted that she wished she had listened to those first instincts, but eventually came to a point where she no longer cared. However, she said she has been working on bettering herself since being convicted and sentenced.

"Being in prison is similar to the prison I put myself in while I was married to Dennis," she said. "However, prison is also what you make of it, so I've enrolled in educational programs, had therapy, and also taken care of myself. Things I should have done in society."

A professional abuser

At a menacing 6'5" and 280 pounds, Dennis Yaklich was a competitive weightlifter who continuously used steroids to supplement his workouts – despite the fact that they also enhanced his aggressive tendencies. While the officers who worked with him conceded that he was always the go-to guy for breaking down a door or clearing a room, he was difficult to manage. In fact, when he did become confrontational, even a supervisor threatened to shoot him because they had no other way to defend themselves.

A former partner once stated that he felt he always had to "clean up after Dennis," and other co-workers have admitted they "dreaded" working with Dennis, because of his aggressive and unpredictable behaviour. Some of his closest colleagues have even confessed that Dennis displayed some "abusive tactics" on the job – while denying the complaints of citizens against him.

Yaklich endured what can only be described as domestic terrorism. While the physical abuse, which included slapping, choking, kicking, and pushing her down stairs as well as sadistic sexual assaults, was indeed disabling and troubling, the psychological abuse was almost worse. According to Yaklich, the threat of death loomed constantly – Dennis would put his gun to her head and threaten to kill her, point his finger at her in the shape of a gun and blow on it after miming shooting her with it, and even beating her under the cover of darkness so she wouldn't be able to prepare for the blows.

The physical abuse has been corroborated by a number of independent witnesses, including a mailman who reported seeing bruises on Yaklich's face, and a telephone repairman who had been called in twice to fix phones after Dennis had yanked them out of the wall in a fit of rage.

Following Yaklich's arrest, the repairman spoke with detectives investigating Dennis' death and said the bruises he had seen on Yaklich's neck and cheek were so prominent, he noticed them "at a glance." The detective inquired how the repairman could recall the incident so vividly, and he admitted that in his line of work, he sees "a lot of things like that in the low income areas and the projects, but I was shocked to see a cop's wife all bruised up like she was."

Cries unheard

Yaklich's first documented attempt for police intervention came in 1982, when she called Dennis' partner to explain that Dennis was "out of control" and threatening to kill her. The detective advised her to leave right away, but she said she was too afraid – if she left, she said, Dennis had told her he would kill her entire family, starting with her father.

Believing that Yaklich was in fear for her life, the detective immediately went to inform his supervisor about the call he'd received about his partner. According to the detective, the supervisor had gestured to indicate that he should just forget the call – it was none of their business – and the incident went unreported.

It was then that Yaklich realized that trying to get help from the police would be completely futile, and she would need to seek support elsewhere.

The next year, in November of 1983, Yaklich endured a short and traumatic visit with a psychologist. After Yaklich "sobbed uncontrollably" through the entire session, the psychologist recommended she leave her husband – but failed to offer her suggestions to muster the courage needed to do so, or what steps she could take to do it safely.

Since Yaklich was required to provide her abusive husband with detailed accounts of where she spent all her time, there was no way for her to continue therapy with regular appointments. She never went back for another session.

A few months later, Yaklich escaped to a battered women's shelter in Denver, in February of 1984. Dennis pleaded with her to come home, and even went so far as to promise that he would try to change – and because she was ashamed to go back to him again, Yaklich told the counselors that she was leaving the state.

Still, the abuse hadn't stopped another year later. Early in 1985, Yaklich tried talking to friends and family members – telling them she needed advice because Dennis was going to kill her. These claims were shrugged off by everyone she turned to, and the abuse began to escalate.

Feeling as though she had no other options, Yaklich began looking for an opportunity to kill herself. Her attempts failed, however, when she realized she would be abandoning her young son and step-children with their abusive father – and after witnessing the struggles of Barbara's children as they grieved the loss of their mother, she was unable to force that situation on her own child.

Later that year, the Pueblo Sheriff's Department received a 911 call from Yaklich's mother. One of the step-children had called Yaklich's parents after hearing what they thought was Dennis pushing Yaklich through a plate glass window. While it turned out that the noise was caused by just a bowl hitting the floor, the officers who responded barely acknowledged Yaklich.

In fact, their inspection of the situation involved a brief conversation with Dennis followed by a tour of the gym Dennis was building on the property. The situation only reinforced Yaklich's desperate situation on the other side of the blue line – living in fear of an abusive spouse with no support or protection from the authorities.

Finally, on December 12, 1985, one of Yaklich's friends finally responded to her pleas for help. A neighbour, Eddie Greenwell, waited at the Yaklich family's farm with his younger brother, Charles, into the early morning hours. When Dennis returned home after working a night shift, the brothers shot and killed him. Yaklich was inside the house, sleeping.

According to court documents, Yaklich had "approached several people" in an attempt to have her husband killed, and had met with Eddie Greenwell many times over a period of eight months. The Greenwell brothers were paid $4,200 in installments after the murder was committed – although the brothers testified they had been promised $45,000.

The story of the tragic marriage was detailed in a made-for-television movie called *Cries Unheard: The Donna Yaklich Story*. The film was released in 1994 and starred former Charlie's Angel Jaclyn Smith as Yaklich.

A disturbing conflict of interest

After Dennis was killed, the Pueblo Police Department – Dennis' employer – carried out an investigation into his death, despite the fact that the murder actually took place in the jurisdiction of the Pueblo Sheriff's Office. Lead roles in the inquiry were awarded to narcotics detectives – Dennis' partners.

The District Attorney was also a personal friend of Dennis', and even admitted to being a material witness in his own case. At the time of the trial, DA Sandstrom was wrapped up in a highly contested election – and this clear political agenda, combined with the attempts of the police department to hide its role in Yaklich's abuse and ultimately, Dennis' death, indicate incredible prejudice against Yaklich from the very beginning.

Not that Yaklich was surprised. After attempting to secure the help of police several times during the course of her abusive marriage, it was obvious to Yaklich that law enforcement was not on her side.

Still, the jury acquitted Yaklich of the charge of first-degree murder. Several jurors even thought Yaklich deserved to be acquitted of all charges, but felt intimidated by the Pueblo Police Department – and feared potential retaliation. Instead, the jury voted guilty on the charge of conspiracy to commit murder, believing that the fair-minded judge would give the battered wife the minimum sentence of eight years.

The probation supervisor who had conducted Yaklich's pre-sentencing investigation testified that Yaklich would be an "excellent candidate" for sentencing alternatives outside of the Department of Corrections, and gave the court his recommendation for the minimum sentence. His testimony affirmed the sense of desperation Yaklich claimed to be struggling with.

"I really felt that whether they did what she wanted done, to have Dennis killed, or whether Dennis found out and killed her, it didn't matter," he said. "She was at a point in her life where either was satisfactory."

However, the late Judge Seavy who presided over the trial chose to overlook the circumstances leading to Dennis' murder and remanded Yaklich to the Department of Corrections for a sentence of forty years. According to the judge, Yaklich "started this whole scenario," and therefore deserved to serve a period of time "in excess of the longest Greenwell's sentence."

"We cannot overlook the fact that Yaklich's participation in the death of her husband was not merely peripheral," stated court documents. "Had it not been for Yaklich, the Greenwells would not have been involved in this murder. Thus, in our view, we would be establishing poor public policy if Yaklich were to escape punishment by virtue of an unprecedented application of self-defense while the Greenwells were convicted of murder."

Still, the jurors were shocked and horrified by the severity of Judge Seavy's harsh sentence. More than half of the serving jurors submitted letters expressing their disappointment with the resulting sentence to a judge who presided over Yaklich's sentencing reconsideration a few years later. These letters were dismissed by that judge, however, who felt "that they must not allow for personal sympathy to influence their decision." Several of the jurors who served on the initial trial event went on to diligently advocate for Yaklich's early release, eighteen years later.

According to Dr. Lenore Walker, who counseled and evaluated Yaklich and provided expert testimony at her trial, Judge Seavy was "using the court and a woman's life to express his own ignorance of a battered woman's plight."

The conspiracy

According to court documents, Yaklich did receive payments totalling more than $250,000 under her late husband's three life insurance policies – leading to a theory that the motivation that pushed her to arrange her husband's death was to obtain this insurance money. The defense argued that Yaklich suffered from "battered woman syndrome," and that the conspiracy to commit murder was a "justifiable act of self-defence ... committed under duress resulting from years of physical and psychological battering by her husband."

"Yaklich lived in a constant state of fear of her husband," the defense argued. "At the time of his death, she believed she was in imminent danger of being killed by him or receiving great bodily injury from him."

The defense went on to explain that many battered women are unable to safely leave their abusive spouses – and in fact, the abuse often escalates as a result of a separation. Abusers have also been known to pursue their victims after they've left, subjecting them to "brutal attacks."

"Additionally, battered women may not psychologically or emotionally have the alternative of leaving the abuser because of their low self-esteem, their emotional and economic dependency, the absence of another place to go, and the woman's legitimate fear of the abuser's response to her leaving," stated the defense. "Battered women become trapped in their own fear and often feel that their only recourse is to kill the batterer or be killed."

Several people involved with the case, including District Attorney Sandstrom, have stated that if Yaklich had gone ahead and committed the murder herself, "she would have walked." However, the DA and many others also question the validity of Yaklich's testimony, including that Dennis was abusing her – maintaining the theory that Yaklich conspired to have him killed just to receive the insurance money.

The DA even stated that "if she had shot him herself, there would be no issue" – leading some to wonder if Sandstrom sees money as an acceptable motive for murder, as long as you follow through with it on your own.

Like most battered women, Yaklich both loved and hated her husband. Killing him herself would have been difficult, as she was afraid that as soon as she pointed a gun at him to save herself and her children, the love she had for him would "override her fear of him," and cause her to second-guess her decision. The ramifications from that could have bene deadly.

Another concern for Yaklich was her husband's established persona of invincibility – one he had carefully instilled in her over years of repeated psychological and physical abuse. Not only did Yaklich struggle to trust in her own ability to kill her husband, she struggled to believe that he would ever really die.

One of the prosecution's expert witnesses, Dr. Alice Brill, said in her testimony that Yaklich didn't meet the traditional profile of a battered woman. These women, according to Brill, generally kill their spouses with little premeditation and show little interest in pursuing relationships with other men – while Yaklich spent at least ten months planning her husband's murder, and had had at least one extramarital affair about a year before Dennis was killed.

Dennis' children also continue to question Yaklich's testimony, stating that none of them had ever witnessed any physical abuse from Dennis during the eight years of the couple's marriage. After Yaklich's parole hearing in October 2005, Dennis' daughter Vanessa fought back tears while talking about the court's decision to release Yaklich after she'd only served eighteen years of her forty-year sentence.

"It's devastating – I don't believe justice has prevailed," she said. "My father died at age 38. He was stripped of his opportunity to live life. He was prevented from raising his children, from seeing us grow up and accomplishing our goals."

Vanessa stated that Yaklich's claims of beatings and abuse were "an outright lie" – and that the depiction of the family's life shown in the TV-movie *Cries Unheard* were based entirely on prison interviews with

Yaklich herself, with no supporting evidence or facts contributed by other relatives or friends.

Vanessa added that just two months before her father was killed, Yaklich had told her that Dennis had asked for a divorce – but that the couple planned to delay the proceedings until after the Christmas holidays, for the sake of the younger children. This story has been corroborated by Dennis' brother, who said Dennis told him over the phone that he planned to divorce Yaklich once the holidays had passed.

"(Dennis') life was taken because he was going to divorce my step-mother and not because she was the victim of abuse," Vanessa said. "I never feared my father, nor did I observe any abuse, whether it be psychological or physical, perpetrated by him. His demeanor was calm and loving, his words encouraging and supportive. I can honestly state my step-mother did not provide my siblings or myself with the same."

According to Vanessa, Yaklich didn't show any grief or remorse after Dennis had been killed – and even slapped Vanessa when she began to cry at her father's funeral. She went on to detail the ongoing "injustice," claiming to defend her father since he is no longer able to defend himself.

"My stepmother's legal defense was paid for by my father's life insurance proceeds and my family and I believe she profited from the made-for-television monstrosity," Vanessa said. "Most recently, her financial status has provided her with the ability to hire a media publicist."

Questions also remain about the relationship Yaklich had with her defense attorney, John Giduck. Records show Giduck and Yaklich took a romantic vacation to Jamaica together prior to her arrest in March 1986 – a getaway funded entirely from the death benefit Yaklich received after having her husband murdered.

In fact, the vacation was cut short when Yaklich was notified of the charges that were being brought against her, and surrendered to police upon her return to Pueblo. Most of the insurance money had already been spent by the time Yaklich was arrested.

According to information reported in the Colorado Springs Gazette, Yaklich had been involved in an extramarital affair about a year before Dennis' murder, and had begun a romantic relationship with Giduck only weeks after her husband's death. Giduck had apparently attended Dennis' funeral, where he had given Yaklich his business card and told him to call if she needed anything.

Yaklich reached out to him a few days later, after police asked her to verify the statement she'd given with a routine polygraph test.

A safe and abuse-free life

Still, Yaklich had a spotless record prior to her incarceration, which continued even after she was sent to prison – a testament to her strength of character. According to prison records, Yaklich managed to vigilantly avoid conflict and strictly followed the many rules surrounding prison life. Despite being forced into an environment filled with trouble, Yaklich managed to stay out of it through her entire eighteen-year term.

During her incarceration, Yaklich obtained an associate's degree as well as a Bachelor's degree in psychology – while working in maintenance and then in a computer-refurbishing program at the correctional facility. According to staff there, Yaklich was a hard and industrious worker, even volunteering her time as a member of the Fire Response Team, comprised of prisoners trained in firefighting and first aid.

Yaklich has also volunteered with several programs that support victims of abuse, earning high praise from her Department of Corrections supervisors regarding the effectiveness of her work with young people. She encourages victims of domestic abuse to seek support from therapy groups to find the strength to break away from an abusive partner – to learn how to stay away emotionally and physically.

"Educating ourselves about the issues and statistics relative to domestic violence will help us pass this information on to the next generation," Yaklich said. "Our children need to learn that they have the right to safe and abuse-free lives."